Decorative Metalworking

Charles P. Holtzman

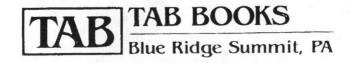

TAB **TAB BOOKS**
Blue Ridge Summit, PA

FIRST EDITION
FIRST PRINTING

©1993 by **TAB Books**.
TAB Books is a division of McGraw-Hill, Inc.

Library of Congress Cataloging-in-Publication Data

Holtzman, Charles P.
　　Decorative metalworking / by Charles P. Holtzman
　　　p.　cm.
　　Includes index.
　　ISBN 0-8306-4267-6 (paper)
　　1. Metal-work.　I. Title.
TT205.B56　1993
684'.09—dc20　　　　　　　　　　92-22207
　　　　　　　　　　　　　　　　　　CIP

Acquisitions editor: Stacy Varavvas-Pomeroy
Book editor: April D. Nolan
Production team: Katherine G. Brown, Director of Production
　　　　　　　　Brenda M. Plasterer, Layout
Index: Kristine D. Lively-Helman
Design team: Jaclyn J. Boone, Designer
　　　　　　Brian Allison, Associate Designer
Cover design: Holberg Design, York, Pa.
Cover photography: Thompson Photography, Baltimore, Md.　　　　HT1

YOU CAN WORK METAL into a great many forms, both decorative and useful. The design possibilities range from tinplate patterns to strip- and sheet-metal projects. The skills and equipment you will need range from the ability to use a few simple hand tools on a table to the skills needed to use heat and more advanced equipment.

This book offers a selection of decorative metalworking projects covering a wide range of designs, techniques, and degrees of skill. There are simple and advanced designs and, in most projects, there are alternatives suggested, so it is possible to vary what you make according to your skill and desires.

You might be interested in making bowls and cups; you might prefer making things from strip metal; your interest might be in blacksmithing or developing sheet-metal shapes. Whatever your main interest, you should find projects here to suit your taste, but I hope you also will attempt to tackle some other aspects of metalwork suggested in these pages.

This is not a book on metalworking techniques. It is assumed you know something about working metal. However, in most projects, guidance on methods and sequence of work is provided to help you if there is something different from your usual experience.

Because this book is a miscellaneous collection of projects covering the whole range of decorative metalworking, the projects are not arranged in order of difficulty or in particular groups. I hope that when you have looked through the whole book, you will have found at least one item that appeals to you immediately and others that will enable you to broaden your skills and produce items that will satisfy your creative instincts and impress your friends with your ability.

In this book, these are the intended meanings of names of metals and alloys:

Soft solder is the lead/tin alloy that can be melted with a hot copper bit, but which in decorative metalworking is more often better melted with a gentle flame.

Brazing is done with a flame using *spelter*, which is a copper/zinc alloy, necessitating raising the work to red heat.

Hard solder is a copper/zinc alloy with one or more other metals added to make the solder melt at a temperature between that of spelter and soft solder.

Tinplate is iron or mild steel sheet coated with thin layers of tin. Steel coated with zinc is sometimes loosely described as *tin*, but that is not what is intended in this book.

Mild steel is iron with a low carbon content. It might be loosely described as *iron*, but pure iron is rare today.

Tool steel is iron with sufficient carbon content to allow it to be hardened and tempered.
Brass is a copper/zinc alloy with a yellow color.

Gilding metal is a copper/zinc alloy with a greater proportion of copper so it has a golden color.

Gunmetal is a name sometimes given to gilding metal, but it is more correctly a copper/tin alloy.

Nonferrous is a term applied to any metal or alloy that does not contain iron.

All sizes quoted are in inches and fractions. There are several gauge sizes used for thicknesses of sheet metal. Where gauge numbers are given in the following pages they refer to U.S. Standard Gauge. Examples are:

> #16g = 0.0625
> #18g = 0.050
> #20g = 0.0375
> #22g = 0.03125

Pot stand

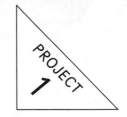

IF YOU HAVE a hand- or-power-piercing saw or fretsaw, pot stands offer scope for working simple or intricate patterns. A pot stand will protect a table surface from hot serving dishes and, when out of use, it serves as a decorative article. Basically, a stand is a sheet of metal mounted on three or four feet. Its openings serve two purposes: to provide the decoration and to disperse heat. A 3-foot stand will work without wobbling, but to keep the surface as flat as possible, four feet is the usual choice. However, if the shape you choose is hexagonal or the cutout is mainly triangular, three feet is more appropriate.

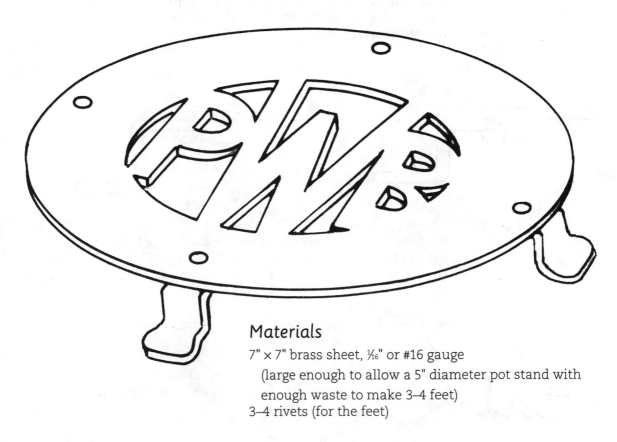

Materials
7" × 7" brass sheet, 1⁄16" or #16 gauge
   (large enough to allow a 5" diameter pot stand with
   enough waste to make 3–4 feet)
3–4 rivets (for the feet)

Pot stand 1

An unlimited scope of individual designs is possible, and you will probably want to modify the patterns suggested or use your own original shapes. If you do, relate the overall size to the pots to be used, and support the top high enough to keep heat from the table—½" will usually be enough.

For most purposes a top diameter of 5" will be satisfactory, and for these instructions that is assumed to be the size. Almost any sheet metal can be used, but brass is particularly appropriate. The metal has to be stiff enough and ⅟₁₆" or #16 gauge should cut without difficulty and have ample strength.

Feet The simplest feet are pieces of the same metal as the top. If you cut your circle from a square, as suggested, you might make the feet from the corner waste metal. For the simplest foot shape, make a double bend and put a countersunk rivet through the top, as shown below. If you think there might be a risk of movement, use two rivets. (See below.)

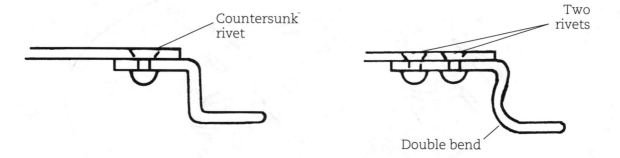

Countersunk rivet

Two rivets

Double bend

Another way to prevent movement with a single rivet is to lightly coat the meeting surfaces with solder and flux, and then heat gently with a small flame after riveting so the solder melts and unites the parts.

What you do with the outlines of the feet depends on the overall design. For many stands, a simple rounding is enough. If the design includes leaves or animals you could use a claw or leaf shape, as shown at left.

2 Decorative Metalworking

Many other feet types are possible, too. With a small dowel to rivet into a hole in the top, you could turn metal feet to any pattern you wish, shown at right. However, keep in mind that not all machining-quality metal is sufficiently ductile to allow riveting without breaking. For this reason, always make a trial piece before turning an entire set of feet.

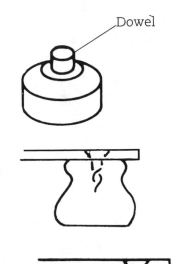

Dowel

The feet for your pot stand need not even be metal. You could turn wood or plastic feet and fix them with wood screws or self-tapping screws, as shown at right. In fact, such feet provide the best heat insulation (which is certainly an asset for this type of project). You could attach metal feet in a similar way, but you would have to tap holes for screws.

Another way to support a metal top is to mount it with screws onto solid wood shown at right. Dark wood showing through polished metal will feature the cutout design by making it more prominent. The wood edge could be square, rounded, or molded.

Getting started

Marking out is best done on paper. When you are satisfied with your drawing, attach the paper to the metal with an adhesive that will hold it securely during the cutting stage, but be sure the paper can be removed when you are finished sawing and drilling. If you are starting with a smooth surface, the paper will prevent accidental damage during working.

If you are making a circular pot stand, use a compass to draw a circle for the outline and another for the border of the pattern. Mark the positions of legs and their rivet or screw holes. After these initial steps, you can concentrate on your chosen pattern.

Design possibilities

As much as possible, make the parts of your pattern link together for mutual support and blend into the border or to each other. If there is a part where this would not be possible without spoiling the design, as at the center of the W in the example shown on page 1, keep it wide for strength. Avoid unsupported fine points.

Initials are possible designs, but think about how certain single letters or combinations will fit into circle pattern. A single bold letter might look better than a group, depending on what you choose. For example, "M" would fit nicely while "I" would look lonely. You can modify a badge or emblem to an outline that would fit in. The inner border does not have to be a circle; you could alter it to fit your chosen badge. Keep in mind, though, that an irregular outline is unlikely to look right. A square, rectangle, octagonal, hexagonal border could contain the design at the center of a circular stand.

By the same token, outlines of stands do not have to be circular. About the only limitation is that, for regular inset patterns, the outsides should be regular shapes. A square with rounded corners or an octagon will suit many designs. If you favor an octagon, though, make sure its outline is accurate, as discrepancies in side lengths will be obvious. The inset pattern in this case will probably be some sort of four-part geometric design, such as the one shown at bottom left.

The six sides of a hexagon can result in some rather acute points. You can ease these and soften appearance by rounding the sides as shown in the center below. The inset pattern could be triangular or six-part geometrically, or it could be something irregular, such as initials.

You could choose to move away from regular outlines, such as with the leaf design shown at bottom right. If you choose to follow this pattern, don't make it too slender or the stand will not be sturdy. This example is drawn over a circle, with veins in the leaf suggested by punched lines.

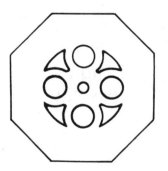  

Some more ideas for cutout patterns are shown on the following page.

4 Decorative Metalworking

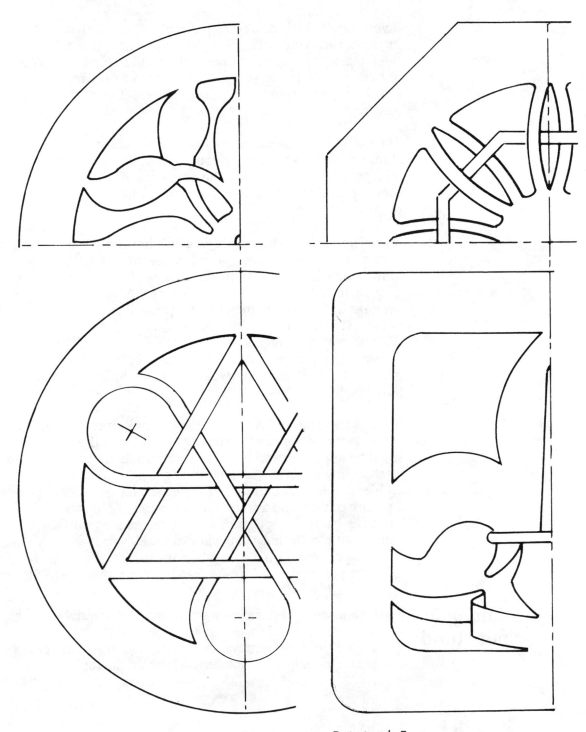

Pot stand 5

If you want to include a pictorial or floral design that differs in its parts, then you will have to draw the whole thing. However, the majority of designs are symmetrical (designed around one or two centerlines), so you will need to draw only half or one-fourth of the pattern and repeat or reverse it to get a balanced picture.

The examples shown here may be used direct to produce stands of reasonable size, or you could scale up by enlarging on a photocopier or drawing squares over the patterns and then repeating the design within larger squares on another piece of paper.

Even if you want to include leaves or other shapes with freehand outlines, you can lay out a design on a half or one-fourth circle if you draw straight symmetrical leaves on the dividing lines (see top left design on page 5). You can indicate overlaps in this case with lightly punched lines.

With an outside octagonal shape, such as the one shown on the top right of page 5, the design can be balanced with an inside octagon. Again, interweaving can be indicated with punched lines.

If the pattern has a three-part theme, a half drawing will allow you to get opposite sides matching. Overlaps in the pattern could be left unmarked or cut in with punched lines to give an intertwining effect (bottom left of page 5). Some badges or emblems will fit into frames of several shapes. You could have a square outline and a frame that is round or elliptical, but there is a balanced appearance if the frame is square inside a square outline. Because you want to avoid very large openings where a pot would tilt, you might have to distort a shape or extend a part of it to fill spaces (see bottom right of page 5).

Finishing your pot stand

Most stands look best if they are polished. You cannot do much to the internal fretted edges, but the saw should have left acceptable surfaces. Remove tool marks from outside edges and polish them at the same time as you do the top surface.

An alternative to a high-polish look is to produce a uniform matte surface. If the metal has been marked, start by polishing it to get it smooth. (With most new sheet metal, this should be unnecessary.)

Using a scouring action in all directions, rub on a fine, abrasive powder with a cloth damped with water or a thin oil, such as kerosene. When the powder is washed off and the metal has dried, you should have a surface without sign of shine that is comparatively non-slip.

Sconce

IN EARLY DAYS, when the only lighting came from candles, it was usual to mount a candle on the wall in a bracket called a *sconce*. To get every bit of useful light from this feeble source, the sconce was often made of tin, because of its good reflective powers.

We do not have much use for candles today, except as ornaments, but a tin sconce and its candle make an effective design feature. An alternative is to fit an electric candle lamp. In that case it would be better to make the sconce of copper or brass. This project, based on a traditional design, is adaptable to both forms. While a copper or brass back will probably be stiff enough unsupported, as shown on page 9 (left), a tinplate back should be stiffened with plywood, as shown on page 9 (right). Both versions are made in basically the same way.

The design shown on page 10 is for a candle about 7" long × 1" diameter (or for an electric candle lamp of the same size). The domed reflector should come behind the flame or lamp filament. If you want to use a candle or lamp of a very different length, adapt the height of the sconce back to suit. Other sizes can remain the same.

Selecting your metal

You will probably have to accept tinplate in whatever thickness is available, which could be #20 gauge or less. It might be possible to cut suitable material from a large can if the inner surface is bright enough for the exposed parts of the sconce. You should be able to cut shapes from tinplate with metal snips.

If you use copper or brass, select sheet material thick enough to hold its shape. This could be #14 or #16 gauge for the back. Other parts could be thinner—#18 or #20 gauge would suit the drip pan and candle holder.

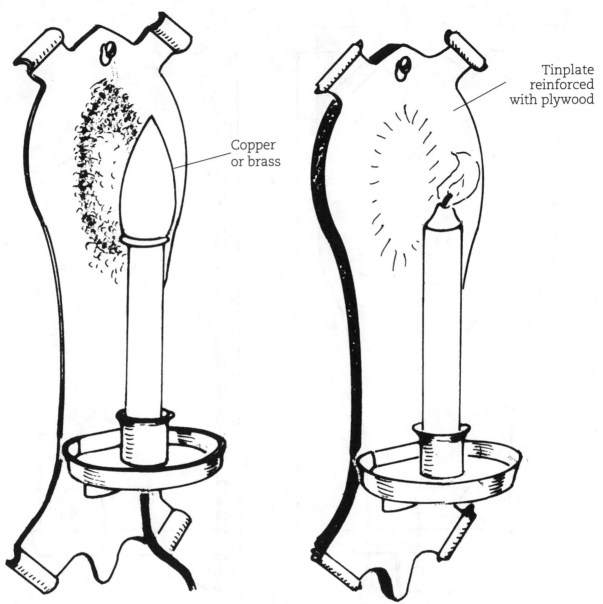

Copper
or brass

Tinplate
reinforced
with plywood

Materials

1 back   8" × 16" × #20 gauge tinplate or #14 or #16 gauge brass or copper

1 drip pan   6" × 6" × #20 gauge tinplate or #18 or #20 gauge brass or copper

1 candle holder   1½" × 6" × #20 gauge tinplate or #18 or #20 gauge brass or copper

1 bracket   1" × 6" × #20 gauge tinplate or #18 or #20 gauge brass or copper

Sconce 9

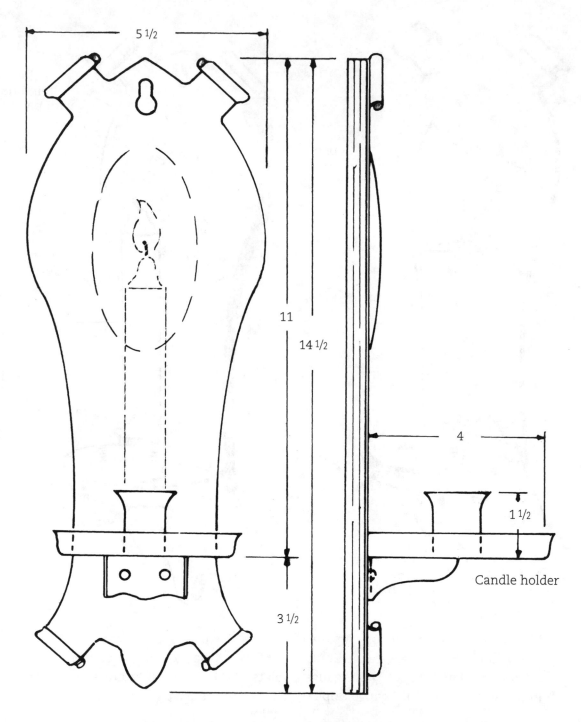

5 1/2

11

14 1/2

4

1 1/2

Candle holder

3 1/2

10 Decorative Metalworking

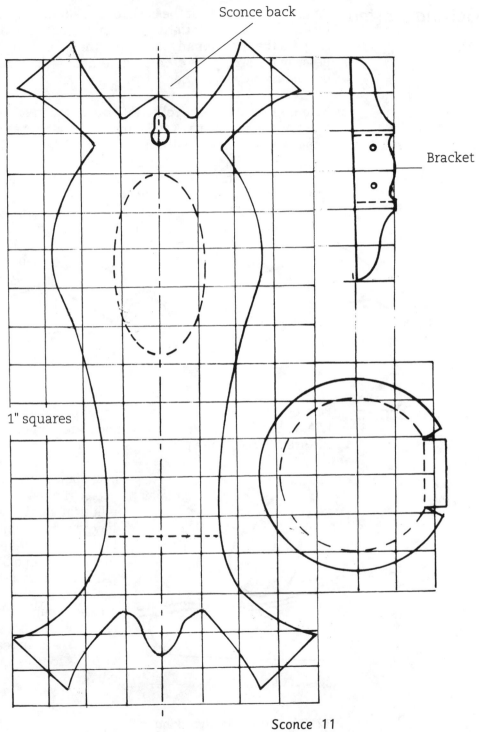

Sconce back

Bracket

1" squares

Sconce 11

Getting started

First, mark out and cut the back to shape following the measurements and pattern shown on page 11. The design's shape is the same for any metal, but the final treatment—and possibly the size of the decorative corners—will be different, depending on your chosen metal.

Because tinplate will be rolled into a scroll with round-nosed pliers, you might want to experiment with a strip of scrap tinplate to see what length will give you a pleasing shape, then cut the back projections to suit (bottom left). The other possible metals are too thick and stiff for the pliers treatment, but they can be bent and then curved back, as shown at bottom right. You might prefer shorter extensions for this treatment.

Thick metal, bent & curved

Rolled tinplate

Making the sconce

Before you begin to make the individual pieces of the sconce, refer to the drawings on pages 10 and 11 for dimensions and the overall look of the project.

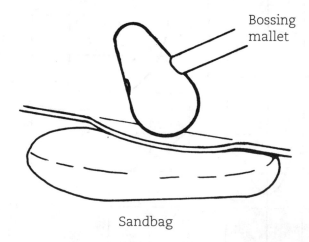

Bossing mallet

Sandbag

The domed reflector should project forward about ¼". It is elliptical, but it does not have a firm outline; it should blend into the flat back. Start by marking an ellipse on the rear surface as a guide, then hollow with a bossing mallet on a sandbag as shown at left. It should not be necessary to anneal copper or brass for this shallow curve.

The sconce back in copper or brass would look attractive if planished all over, but you could planish the dome only as an alternative and let the hammer marks blend into the smooth surrounding surface as shown at right.

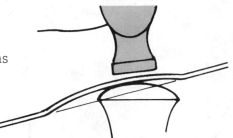

The candle holder is made from a parallel strip 1½" wide rolled to fit the candle or candle lamp base. With tinplate, be sure to allow for overlapping the meeting ends ⅛", as shown at bottom left and join with soft solder. On the other hand, you can cut copper or brass to meet and then join the sides with hard solder, as shown at bottom right. Flare the top by hammering over a rounded stake as shown at right.

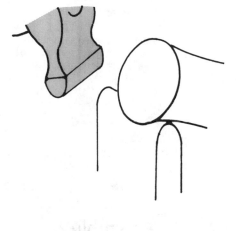

The drip pan is circular, except for a flat part at the back. Cut the shape, allowing ½" to turn up. To get an even shape, cut a wood former to the inner outline and another piece to go outside as shown at top of following page. Grip the metal between these blocks in a vise or with a clamp and hammer over the edge, moving around a little at a time. You might hammer directly onto the metal, or you could use a piece of hardwood as a punch. Tinplate will wrinkle, but you can regulate the pattern to give an attractive deckle edge.

You should be able to turn over brass or copper to a smooth edge, although you might have to anneal intermediately. In any metal, the rim need not finish upright—providing the flare is even—but make the straight back square.

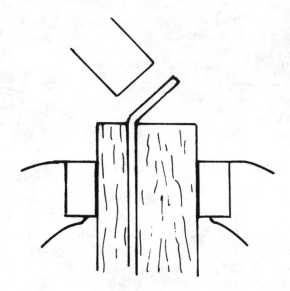

The bracket has double arms. Cut its shape (referring to the illustration on page 11) and fold it squarely. In tinplate, you can drill for small screws to go through the plywood back. In other metal, drill for ⅛" rivets.

Assembly & finishing

If you will be using an electric candle lamp, drill through the center of the drip pan for the wire. As you drill, allow enough room for a rubber or plastic grommet, which will serve to remove any risk of chafing. Soft solder the candle holder to the top of the drip pan and the bracket to the underside. Soft solder the back of the drip pan to the sconce back, and drill through the bracket holes.

It will probably be worthwhile to polish the separate parts before completing the assembly, but on any pieces where you will be soldering, be sure to scrape the surface clean of polish residue. You can brighten tinplate by rubbing it with fine whiting or chalk powder. The other polished metals could be lacquered.

If you need to stiffen a tinplate back, cut thin plywood to the back shape, and stain its edges black. Then join the tinplate to the plywood with epoxy glue or fine pins.

Parallel pots

SIMPLE AND PLEASING containers can be made by rolling sheet copper into cylinders, joining the edges, and attaching bottoms. You can then decorate these containers in a variety of ways, including the twisted-wire embellishment suggested in this project. If you keep to a uniform design, a set of containers in different shapes can be attractive.

Materials

container
    sheet copper #18 gauge

embellishment
    copper wire #16 gauge

The sheet copper you use can be almost any thickness, but #18 gauge is perhaps most suitable, with copper wire of about #16 gauge. Proportions look best in this type of container if height and diameter are different, as shown on page 15. You can make a general-purpose pot such as (left), broaden into a shallow tray (middle), or build upwards to make a vase (right)—which could be given handles.

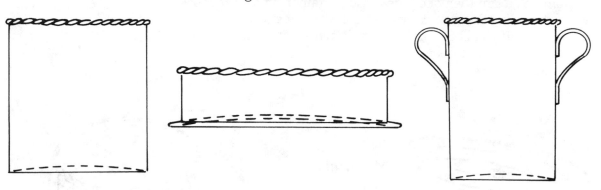

Making the cylinder

Start with a square-ended strip that is a little longer than three times the intended diameter. (Precision in the final diameter is rarely essential.) Roll the metal into a cylinder by pressing or hitting the sheet over wood or metal of a smaller diameter, as shown at right. If you do not get a perfect cylinder at this stage, it doesn't matter; you can true the shape after you join the edges.

Metal

File the meeting edges to form a V open on the inside. Use soft iron wire around the cylinder to draw the joint close. Put a few pieces of hard solder, with flux, on the joint, and heat with a propane or other flame until the joint is made (as shown on top left of next page). Clean the cylinder inside and out.

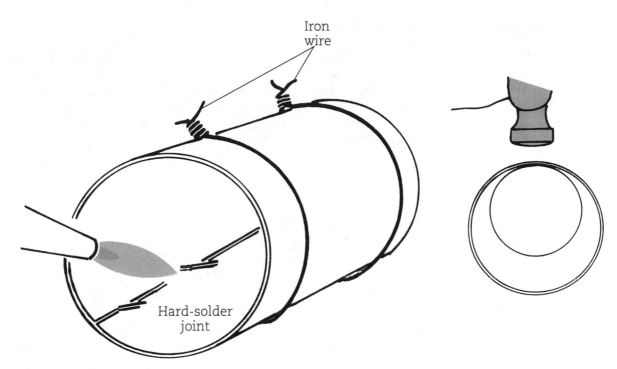

Iron wire

Hard-solder
joint

Next, true the cylinder shape, if necessary. Planish all over with a slightly domed hammer on a steel rod (above right). True the ends by filing or rubbing them on sheet abrasive paper supported on a flat surface.

The bottom could be a flat disc, but the container will stand better if it is hollowed out, even if only slightly. Cut a disc a little too big and dome it less than ¼" with a bossing mallet on a sandbag. There should be no need to planish it.

Wire the bottom in place as shown below. Put small pieces of soft solder inside the joint with some flux. Heat gently around the outside to draw the molten solder through. Level the bottom edge to the cylinder (right). If you prefer, you can extend the base, as shown for the tray, preferably making it hollow.

Fitting the bottom

Iron wire

Solder

Twisted wire decoration

Twisted wire around the top of the container both decorates it and stiffens the rim. To achieve this embellishment, cut a length of wire a little more than twice the circumference of the cylinder. Anneal it and clean it, then loop it around a peg in a vise. Grip the two ends in the chuck of a hand drill, and tension and twist the wire as shown below. You can adjust the amount of twist, but be careful not to make it too tight or the wire will snap. A hand drill is necessary for this operation because an electric drill does not give you enough control.

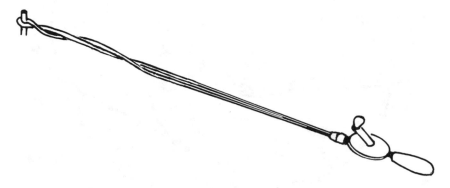

Next, bend the twisted wire into a circle and cut the meeting ends to the outside angle of the twist (left). Make a circle that will be just too small to press onto the pot, joining the ends with hard solder. Lightly hammer the ring over a steel rod, progressing around until you have stretched it enough to press on. Join this ring to the rim with soft solder. Finish the pot by polishing all over.

Handles & lids

If you want to put handles on a vase, you can use strips of copper that are thick enough to be stiff, but the handles will look better if they are made of thin metal with rolled edges as shown at right. For each handle cut a strip ¾" or ⅞" wide. Anneal it, if necessary, and fold the edges over a strip of wood or metal ½" wide as shown at the top left of the next page. Complete folding it in with a mallet so you are left with a rounded edge as shown at the top right of the next page.

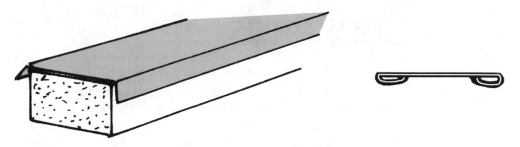

Shape the handles over a ¾"-diameter rod. (Make sure the two handles match.) Hollow the handles to fit against the cylinder, then wire them in place and soft-solder them. Scrape off any surplus solder, and polish all over.

You can make a lid for a pot by attaching a ring to a disc (below). Use a strip of sheet metal ¼" wide to make a ring to fit easily into the pot. Cut a disc to overlap the top of the pot, and dome out its center. Wire the parts together, and join them with soft solder.

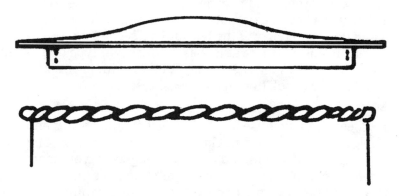

Bookends

IF YOU WANT to hold books upright and in place when there are not enough of them to fill the shelf, a simple bent piece of sheet metal is all you need. Such *single-angle* bookends would be almost out of sight; decoration would be inappropriate, and there would be no need for polish. The bottom should be long enough to go under two or three books, so that the weight of the books provides stability as shown at the top left of opposite page. One advantage of this type of bookend is that a pair do not add to the length of the row, so you can have books arranged almost up to the maximum space available.

An alternative is a pair of basically similar bookends designed to be used on a desk or table where they would be seen as shown on the bottom of the next page. In this case, the upright parts are decorated and polished or painted, and the bases of the bookends become part of the design since they will not be completely hidden under the books. This second type of bookend forms a *T-shape* at its base. Whichever type of bookend you choose, sizes suggested will suit books with page sizes up to those of this book (top right, opposite page).

Single-angle bookends

The sheet metal you use for this project should be stiff enough to hold its shape. A good thickness would be between #14 gauge and #22 gauge. If you intend to do piercing work, you might prefer thinner metals. As a guideline, remember that steel is usually thinner than brass, and brass is usually thinner than copper or aluminum.

Design possibilities

For decoration you can shape the outline only, pierce a pattern with a fretsaw, or do both. Most decoration is appropriate in the upper half of the bookend. Do not cut out so much that stiffness is reduced. Usually, a broad border will provide rigidity.

Some possible designs are suggested in the following pages. Although two bookends should be treated as a pair, they need

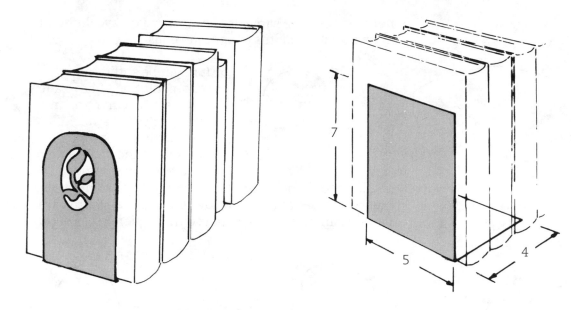

Materials

Single-angle bookends (pair):
   5" × 13" sheet metal, #14–#22 gauge

T-shaped bookends (pair):
2 bottoms   5" × 9"
2 support   5" × 10"

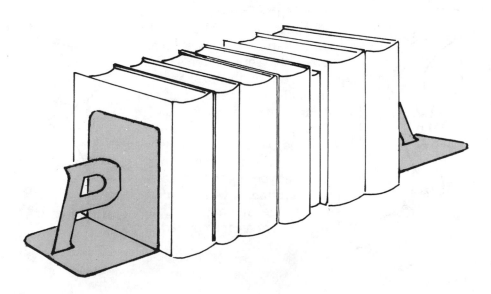

not be exactly the same design. You could have different initials or other motifs at opposite ends.

It might be sufficient ornamentation to have a few symmetrical curves or an arrangement of straight lines, such as those shown at left. On the other hand, curves do not have to be symmetrical. For boating books, for example, you could shape some stylized breaking waves as shown below left. Another alternative is to pair a geometric outline with geometric piercing as shown below right.

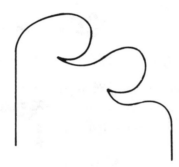 

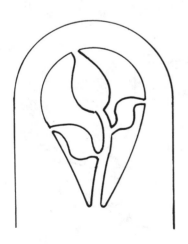

Although the framing of a cutout might be symmetrical, it could include natural shapes, such as leaves (left). For children's books, it might be possible to shape almost all of the depth of an end into an animal (right). If you choose such a shape, be sure to avoid sharp corners or points with any external shape, but keep in mind that you might have to ease off with rounding what would be sharp on the animal (such as a bird's beak or a cat's pointed ear).

Initials are obvious choices. You could shape them on the tops of the ends as outlines, or you could include them in frames, as shown at right. You could use single letters or arrange them as monograms. Much depends on how the particular letters can be made to fit the border.

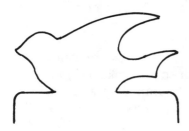

If the sheet metal you have chosen seems barely stiff enough and you do not want to risk weakening it with much shaping and piercing far down, you can choose a design that occupies only the top edge, as shown at left.

Finishing single-angle bookends

Single-angle bookends should look attractive with plain surfaces. If you have used copper or brass, you could planish the bookends using a round-faced hammer. The resulting pattern of indentations will give the metal a sumptuous look when polished. You will need to planish before shaping or piercing so that cut edges will not be distorted as they might be if planishing followed cutting.

Bending should come last, after all other work. Bend the metal to a tight fold and check that the faces are exactly at 90° to each other.

If sharpness is taken off edges and corners, the bookends should not damage polished tabletops, but they might slide and cause scratches. You can reduce this risk by gluing cloth (felt works well) to the undersides of the bookends.

T-shaped bookends

The single-angle bookends just described are not very obvious in use. If you want to make bookends that are more decorative in themselves, you can extend them outwards, as shown at the bottom of page 21. The ornamental parts are then square to the

row of books. The basic T-shaped assembly is functional, and the decoration is added in the form of a bracket as shown at left.

You can use any of the sheet metals specified for the first type of bookends, or you could mix metals by making ornamental parts from a different metal than the main parts. There is some advantage in appearance in using thicker metal for the shaped pieces, but if your equipment will not profile thicker metal, these parts could be thin. Profiled pieces ⅛" thick look more attractive than thinner ones.

The basic parts form a T-shaped assembly as shown below. The outer corners should be rounded. For some bookends you might wish to shape the outlines, but parallel parts do not detract from focus on the ornamental parts.

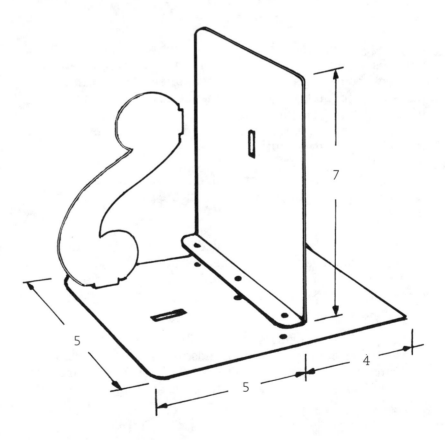

When you design your own decorative pieces, be sure to allow for flat parts, square to each other, to fit against the main parts. The tenons can be ½" across and only just long enough to reach the other sides of their slots.

As with the single-angle bookends, a very large number of decorative designs are possible with the T-shaped option. Besides the scroll shown at the bottom of page 24, you can cut figures of people, trees, foliage or flowers. You could use a pair of initials tilted inwards as shown below (left) or one of the ornate patterns often used on shelf brackets as shown below (right).

Design possibilities

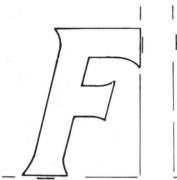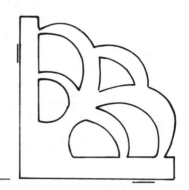

Another possibility is to take the outline of something long and halve it, so you put part of it at each end as shown below. The extended parts of a fish shown here is but one version. Another clever design would be an arrow that apparently goes through the books. Many animals and birds are possible, but you might have to adjust postures to get suitable bearings on the main parts. An example is the duck with its head turned back, as shown at right.

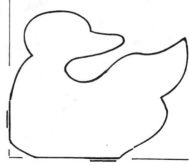

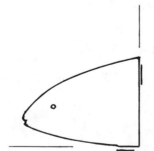

Assembly of T-shaped bookends

Bend the bottom of the upright part squarely for ¾" to take three ⅛" rivets as shown at the bottom of page 24, which can be roundhead on top and countersunk underneath. Cut and drill the base to match. When you assemble the project, it should be sufficient to rely on the rivets only. If necessary, though, you can soft-solder brass or copper.

Join the decorative pieces with tenons into slots. Cut the slots as shown so the tenons fit easily.

Rivet the main parts together. Try the tenons in place and check to ensure the faces that will come against a book are square. If not, adjust the tenon parts to suit. Soft solder the tenons in their slots. Be careful not to melt too much solder. Put flux in a joint. Heat with a small flame, and then touch the end of a stick of solder briefly to the open side when you judge the heat is sufficient.

Finish by polishing or planishing, and glue cloth underneath as described for the single-angle bookends.

Pastry cutters

DO YOU KNOW a cook who might want to cut rolled-out pastry into various shapes? If so, you can provide the means of producing individual shapes different from the standard patterns you can buy in a store. In this project, the decorative work is in the product it produces, not in the metalwork itself (see below).

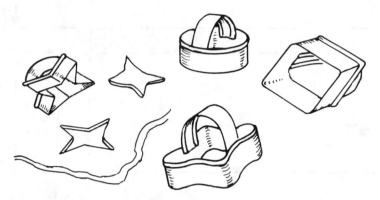

Materials

The amount of tinplate you will need depends on how many cutters you plan to make and on what their sizes will be. If you are careful in marking and cutting out, you can easily make all the shapes shown above with one 15" × 15" sheet of tinplate.

The ideal material for pastry cutters is tinplate. You might be able to cut suitable metal from an unpainted can, but slightly thicker sheet is preferable for most cutters. Tinplate edges as cut will be sharp enough to cut pastry, but you should protect all other edges by folding. All joints are made with soft solder.

Whatever the shape, the technique of making a pastry cutter is basically the same. Your cook will probably want round cutters in several sizes and the making of one will serve as an example for the others (see right).

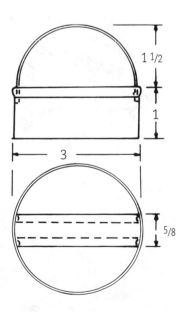

Marking out & folding

You can standardize the width of folded edges at ¾₆" or ¼". Do not mark out tinplate with a steel scriber; doing so will scratch through the tin coating and expose the steel to rust. Instead, mark the tinplate with a pencil or a *brass scriber,* which is a piece of stout brass wire filed to a point.

First, cut a strip long enough to form the circle. Mark the fold and tab for the joint as shown below. As in all the following shaped cutters, if the strip is too long, you can trim it after shaping.

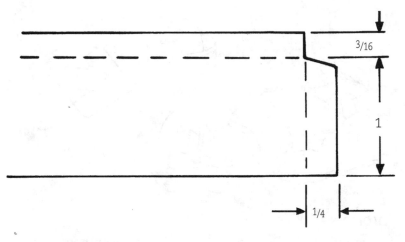

3/16

1

1/4

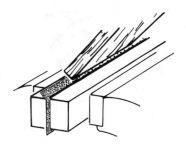

Start the fold by hammering it squarely. If you do not have folding bars, hold the tinplate between stiff metal strips in a vise as shown at left. Using a piece of wood as a punch allows you to get a smoother fold than you would get by using a mallet directly. Close down the fold on a flat surface as shown at bottom left, and roll the strip to shape over a round metal rod or a turned block of wood. Solder the tab inside and, if neccessary, true the shape.

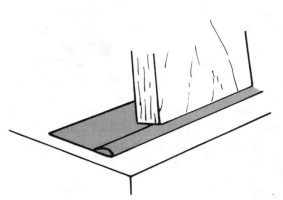

Cut a strip for the handle, allowing for both edges to be folded as shown below. Turn both edges squarely. All handles will be the same width, regardless of the shape of the cutter, so you can standardize on one bending strip, as shown at right, to use with another behind it in a vise.

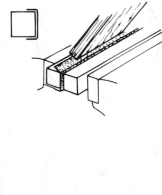

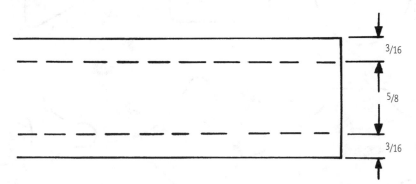

3/16

5/8

3/16

Close down the folds and bend the handle to shape. Try it in the cutter and trim it to a length that allows no more than ⅜" overlap. Solder the handle in place square to the ring joint to keep the heat of the soldering away from the first joint.

Of course, handles are an option. In fact, the cook might prefer to have some shapes unhandled. Very small pastry cutters, such as those used to cut parts out of already shaped pieces, are better without handles.

Special shapes

You can use your own ideas for special shapes. Some ideas are shown in the illustration on the following page. The main rule of thumb is to avoid acute angles and sharp corners since pastry will usually break up if formed in such shapes. You could bend corners over a hatchet stake, but it might be better to make a small stake to hold in a vise, with a slightly rounded acute-angled edge as shown on page 31 (left). For places where a more moderately curved corner will do, make a stake with a rounded top as shown on page 31 (right). In both cases have the stake wider than the metal to be bent and smooth the bearing surface to prevent damage to the tinplating.

On most angular designs joints are best arranged at corners. Geometric outlines are popular and good choices, while animal

For curled pastry

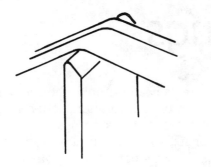
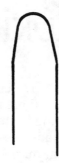

or leaf shapes cannot be precise because you must avoid sharp corners and acute angles. For patterns with holes in them, it is better to make one cutter for the outline and another for the hole. Don't try to make a combined cutter for a one-action press.

Not all cut pastry shapes are destined to remain flat. You can make an extended cutter to suit what will be a curled shape. Another can have extensions to allow for parts of the pastry that are to be crimped or turned in. Pastry does not respond to closely curved deckle edges. Arrange moderately curved undulations rather than saw-tooth edges.

Finishing

When you are through folding and working your cutters, wash them to remove flux. Polish with whiting or chalk powder to brighten and remove any surface grease; then wash again before putting into use.

Napkin rings

RINGS FOR TABLE NAPKINS are basically simple, short lengths of tube, but there is room for plenty of decoration, both on surfaces and in shape as shown below. Napkin rings are usually made in sets of four or six, so be prepared to repeat a design that number of times. Choose a pattern that can be worked several times rather than just once. If you make a set, it is advisable, for the sake of uniformity, to do the same stage of work on each ring in turn and not make complete rings one at a time.

Materials
1 piece   8" length seamless tubing, 2" diameter, #16–#20 gauge
or 1 piece 8" × 8" length

A ring should be 1½" to 2" diameter (or the equivalent in other shapes). A width of ⅞" to 1¼" should suit most needs.

If you can find tubing of a suitable diameter, almost any metal can be used. Stainless steel, copper, brass, or any alloy that can be polished should look attractive as plain rings. Even iron piping could be used and finished by painting. If possible, true the cut ends on a lathe; otherwise, do it by filing.

If you have to make a ring by shaping and then joining the ends of a strip, you are limited to copper, brass, and the alloys that can be hard-soldered. It might be possible to rivet the overlapping ends of other metals, but in this shape it is difficult to do neatly.

Seamless tubing of suitable size is usually fairly thick. If you want to make a ring from sheet copper or brass, it can be #16 gauge to #20 gauge. The thinner metal is suitable for the turned edges described as follows.

Rings from tubing

A plain ring cut from a tube could be decorated with an overlay such as the one shown below. A good idea for this type of decoration is an initial or a symbol that would identify a person's place at the table, for example.

You could fit it with soft solder, but this will almost certainly result in some excess to be scraped away. To avoid such a problem, use epoxy adhesive. Make sure the parts fit closely and are clean; then lightly coat both surfaces and clamp them together. You can bend a cotter pin for use

as a clamp as shown at right. Most epoxy adhesives have to be left for about three days to build up strength. Be sure you allow enough time so that the joint will be as strong and waterproof as solder.

Rings from sheet metal

If you are making a ring from a strip, you can cut out initials or symbols before bending as shown below. Remember, though, that the fretsawing has to be small and fine; be sure to choose bold outlines and avoid complications such as intertwined initials.

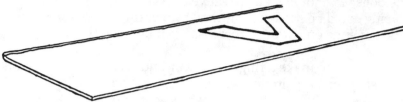

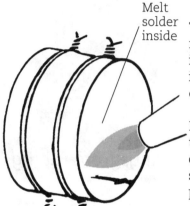

Melt solder inside

To make a ring from sheet metal, cut a strip about 1" × 5" and roll it into a circle. File the meeting ends slightly V-shaped inside, and tie with pieces of soft iron wire. Melt hard solder inside, as shown at left. The heat will anneal the metal so you can shape it easily.

Instead of a circle, you could follow the same general directions to make an elliptical shape as shown below (right). Planish all over to decorate and harden the metal. You can leave the edges slightly uneven from planishing or trued by filing before final polishing.

Design & decoration options

A napkin ring does not have to be circular or elliptical. For example, you could include a flat part on an otherwise circular shape to prevent the napkin ring from rolling off the table as shown below (left). Such an addition would also serve to keep the design mark facing up.

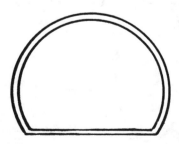

Another alternative is to make up the whole shape of flat surfaces, such as with a hexagonal or octagonal ring as shown at the top of the following page. To do this, mark the positions of the bends on the strip, and bend the strip over an angular edge as shown at top right of page 35. Make the joint at a corner. (A drawing or a template will help you get an even shape.)

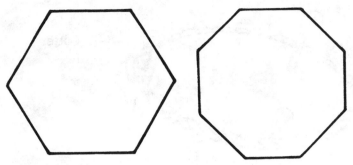

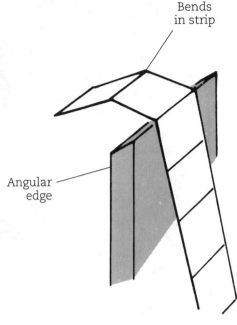

Bends
in strip

Angular
edge

A ring of any section, in lighter metal, can be decorated, stiffened, and made easier for threading a rolled-up napkin through, if the edges are belled out over a small rounded stake as shown below. The amount of curving of the edge need not be great, but it should at least be even.

Yet another decorative option is to add twisted wire to the edges of a plain round or elliptical ring as shown at right. Prepare it in the same way as suggested for

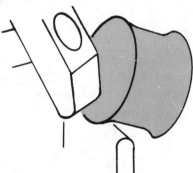

project 3, following the instructions and illustrations on page 18.

Make the twisted wire rings a tight fit by bending cotter pins to prevent movement as shown

Twisted
wire

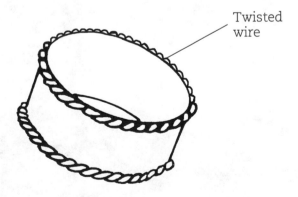

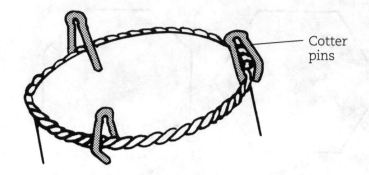

Cotter
pins

above. Soft-solder both of the twisted wire rings at the same time.

Small bowls

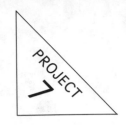
BECAUSE COPPER IS THE MOST ductile of the common metals, it is also the most suitable for hollowing. Gilding metal will hollow almost as well as copper, and it finishes with a golden sheen. Brass, on the other hand, is not so easy to shape. If you keep in mind which metals work best for hollowing, you can easily form small bowls. You will need to use only simple equipment, and you can finish your projects in a variety of ways as shown below.

Materials

Bowls: copper or gilding metal, #20 gauge
Bases: copper or gilding metal, #14 or #16 gauge or ⅛" × ⅜" strip

Annealing & hollowing

In making your bowls, you will need to anneal several times. This work can be done with a propane torch of modest size or even on an iron plate over a gas burner. Your annealing facilities, however, might limit the size of hollowed work you can tackle. The metal has to reach red heat.

Before you begin your project, cut a disc of #20 gauge metal 4" to 5" diameter and anneal it. After each annealing, clean the metal with pumice powder or a domestic cleaning powder and water. Without regular cleaning, you might find difficulty in getting an even polish due to discoloration on the surface.

To hollow, use a bossing mallet over a sandbag or over a depression in the end grain of a log. You will probably find working over a wood depression gets quicker results as shown below (left), but it is easier to get an even shape on a sandbag as shown below (right). Work in circles from the center outward so that the blows overlap.

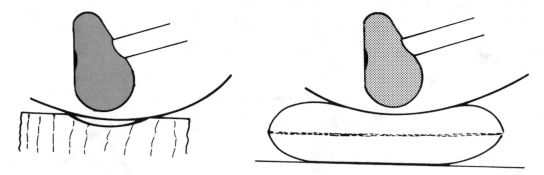

When the metal shows that it has hardened by its limited response to mallet blows, anneal again. Continued hitting after the metal has hardened will serve no purpose and, in an extreme case, could result in breaking through the metal.

Making the bowl shape

A near-semicircular section of metal is easy to obtain by following the annealing/hollowing process described (see far left). An elliptical section results from doing more work toward the rim as shown below (left). You could continue working there to almost turn in the rim as shown below (right), but that is usually appropriate only for larger bowls.

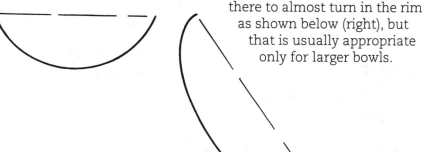

Invert the bowl on a flat surface to check that it is symmetrical and that the rim is flat. You might have to do some local hitting to true the shape, but minor inequalities will be trued when you planish. You also might need to file high spots off the rim. However, final leveling is best done on a piece of abrasive paper on a flat surface—pressing and rubbing with a circular action.

Planish over a mushroom stake so hammer marks overlap each other. Work in circles from the center outward and pinch the metal each time between the hammer and stake as shown at right. Round the edge, and then check that the rim is still true when the bowl is inverted on a flat surface.

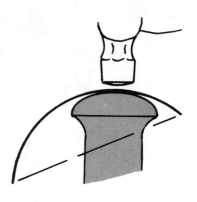

Parallel bases

The simplest base is the parallel ring shown below. It could be a section cut from a tube, but you will probably have to bend a strip to size. Use metal thicker than for the bowl (#14 gauge or #16 gauge if possible). Join the ends with hard solder. You could planish the ring, but that might not be worthwhile, unless hardening by hammering is advisable.

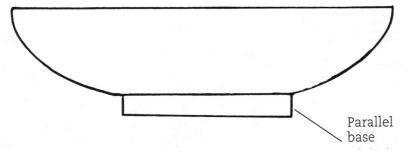

Parallel base

Locate the base centrally on the inverted bowl and tie it on with soft iron wire as shown at the top left of the next page. Put flux and small pieces of soft solder inside the ring and heat gently with a small flame as shown at the top right of the next page to melt and draw the solder through. Alternatively apply flux, then heat, to what you judge to be the melting point of soft solder and touch the end of the stick of solder very briefly inside the ring so enough of it melts and makes the joint.

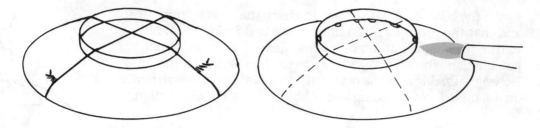

If necessary, scrape off any excess solder and level the bottom by rubbing on flat abrasive paper. Polish all over.

Tapered bases

A tapered base might be considered more attractive as shown in the illustration below. Its shape is part of a cone and you have to form it in two stages. Draw a side view and continue the sloping lines to reach a point; then use a compass to draw curves through the ends of the drawn base. Measure round this a little more than three times the intended diameter, as shown in the illustration at the bottom.

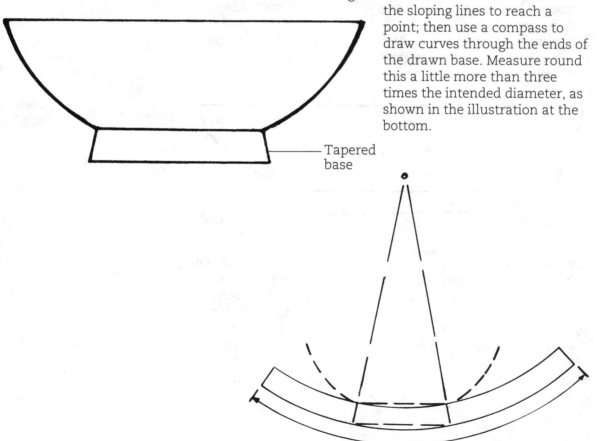

— Tapered base

Next, cut a piece of sheet metal to this shape. Bend it to a circle, and join the ends with hard solder. Join the ring to the bowl in the same way as the plain ring.

If a shallower, tapered base is what you want, you could bend strip instead of cutting a shape from sheet metal. Use a piece of bar not bigger than ⅛"-×-⅜" section. Anneal it and bend it to the developed curve shown at right. Make it into a ring in the same way as with the sheet metal base and solder on in the same way.

You can make a flared base by raising from a disc with a hole as shown below. Make the disc about half the diameter of the bowl and cut a hole not more than half that diameter as shown below (right). Anneal the metal.

Flared bases

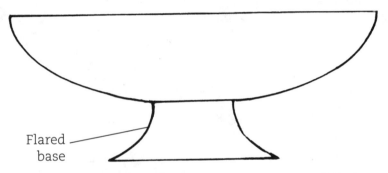

Flared base

Have the metal hooked over a bick iron or a steel rod held in a vise. Tilt the metal and use a raising mallet or hammer, working in circles outward from the hole to stretch the metal around the hole as shown below. Do not hammer too much near the rim. As the work progresses, tilt the work toward the tool as shown below (right). Anneal frequently or you might cause the metal to crack at the hole. Continue until you have a shape that is pleasing when put under the bowl. If necessary, trim the shape so the rim stands flat.

You will probably have to do some filing at the top to get it parallel to the bottom. When this is satisfactory, planish from outside with a well-rounded hammer as shown at left. Fit the base to the bowl on a flat surface to see if the bowl rim will be level. Then wire the base to the bowl, and soft-solder in the same way as the other bases. Polish all over.

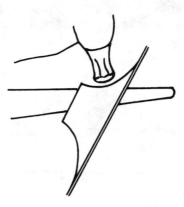

Broad-based vases

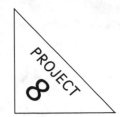

FOR A FLOWER VASE to stand firmly, it needs a broad or heavy base. This vase design satisfies both requirements. The weight of water in the broad base helps prevent the vase from tipping.

Two sizes are suggested, but you are certainly free to use other sizes as shown below and at the top of the next page. A pair of vases would look even more effective than one. If you do decide to make more than one vase, work on both at the same time, rather than completing them one at a time. In that way, you ensure that the two vases are the same, and you will probably save time.

Materials
#18 gauge copper, brass, or gilding metal.

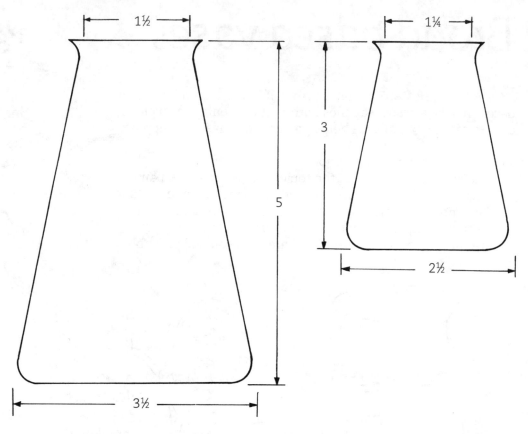

Use copper sheet about #18 gauge. Brass or gilding metal should shape almost as readily. Finishing with chromium or other plating would improve appearance, although you might prefer to lacquer polished metal.

Making the body

You have to develop the opened-out shape of the body. Sizes for the developments of the suggested vases are shown; those for the smaller vase are in parentheses as shown at the top of the next page. If you have to develop other sizes, draw a side view and continue the side lines until they meet, and use that as your compass center.

If you do not have a compass large enough, you can improvise one with a strip of wood, a nail, and a pencil as shown at the bottom of the next page. To be exact, the distance around the curve should be 3½ times the diameter, but precision is not

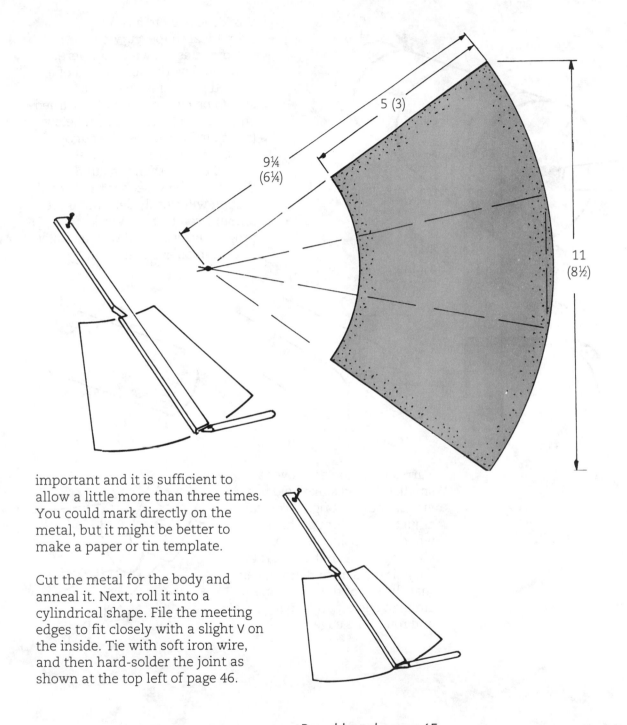

5 (3)

9¼
(6¼)

11
(8½)

important and it is sufficient to
allow a little more than three times.
You could mark directly on the
metal, but it might be better to
make a paper or tin template.

Cut the metal for the body and
anneal it. Next, roll it into a
cylindrical shape. File the meeting
edges to fit closely with a slight V on
the inside. Tie with soft iron wire,
and then hard-solder the joint as
shown at the top left of page 46.

Broad-based vases 45

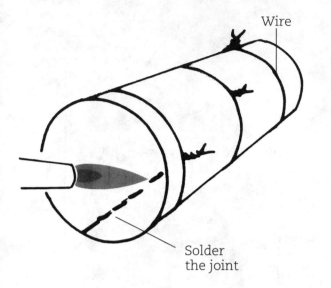

Wire

Solder
the joint

Work the body to a good cylindrical shape, curving the bottom in as shown below (left). You could work over the end of a shaped piece of hardwood as shown below (center) or the turned end of a steel rod as shown below (right). In both cases, the curve around the stake or mandrel should be less than the curve of the end of the vase, but the curved section will closely determine the amount you turn in. Work progressively around with a mallet to turn in an even amount.

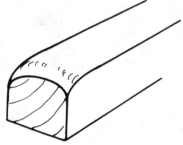

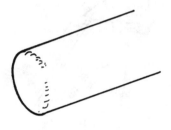

Turn out the top edge over a small, rounded stake held in a vise as shown at right. You can adjust the amount of this lip to what you consider to be a pleasing shape, but see that the curve is the same all around and that the top of the vase remains circular. File off any inequalities and round the edge.

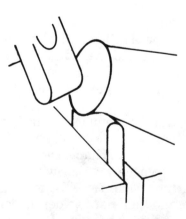

Planish all over, using a steel rod as large as will fit in as a stake. Level the lower edge so it will make a close fit on the bottom as shown at right. You might have to file off high spots, but you can get the surface true by rubbing with a circular motion on abrasive paper resting on a flat surface.

Cut a disc for the bottom a little bigger than the edge of the body. Wire it on and soft solder it in place with a torch flame and no more heat than necessary to make the solder run into the joint. File the disc as shown below so it follows the body curve.

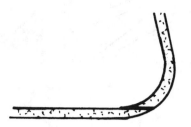

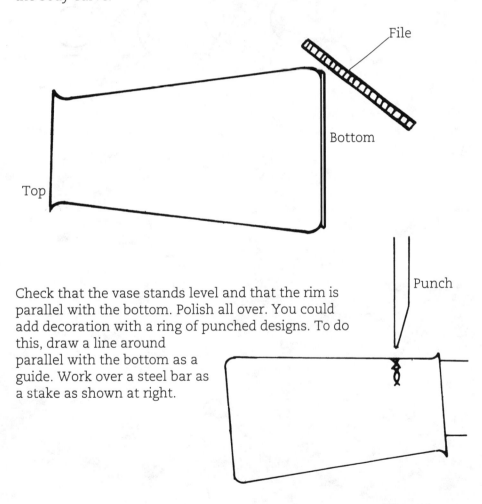

File

Bottom

Top

Punch

Check that the vase stands level and that the rim is parallel with the bottom. Polish all over. You could add decoration with a ring of punched designs. To do this, draw a line around parallel with the bottom as a guide. Work over a steel bar as a stake as shown at right.

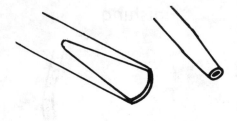

You can combine a few simple marks such as those made by half-moon punches and circle punches as shown at left. A few patterns are suggested here as shown below.

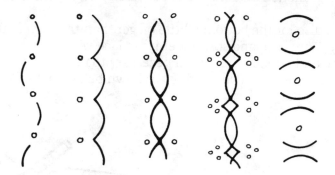

Hinges

FOR MANY PURPOSES, a plain manufactured hinge is all you need. As a metalworker, though, you can make hinges that are both decorative and functional. You can make hinges in many sizes: from those on small boxes to those on chests, yard gates, and house doors. If you want to make a hinge for a metal box, you can incorporate the hinge in the same piece of metal as the box. In the past, when hinges had to be made individually, the hinge knuckle had more than just its two plain flaps to take screws, nails or rivets; the flaps were often extended and decorated. Hinges on old buildings or antique furniture can provide you with ideas for making modern hinges. In addition, some design ideas are provided here.

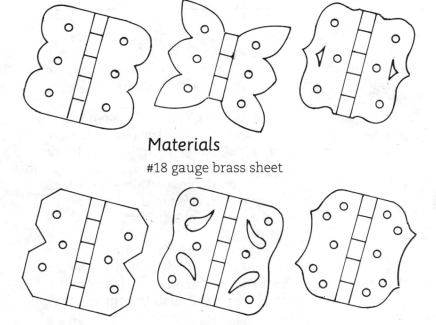

Materials
#18 gauge brass sheet

Hinges are usually needed in pairs. For double doors you might need four, while for a heavy door you might need three. Make all you need at one time, working stages in step on each to ensure uniformity.

Making knuckles

The knuckle, as the functional part of the hinge, must be properly made and able to continue use without failing, so accurate construction is important. A knuckle is made with an uneven number of parts. There could be three, as shown below (left), but five is more typical as shown below (center) and a broad hinge could have more. In most hinges the parts are of equal width, but for a better share of the load, the two knuckles on one side could be wider than the three on the other as shown below (right). If there are differences, it is usual for the outer parts to be on the short part of the hinge.

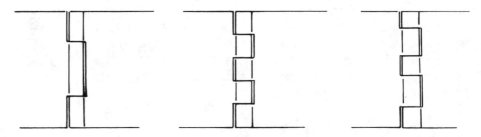

If you want to experiment with forming a hinge knuckle, choose a medium size such as ³⁄₁₆" pin and #18 gauge brass sheet. The formation of the hinge knuckle is the same for any size, but this test will allow you to observe the technique.

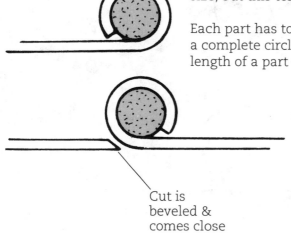

Cut is beveled & comes close

Each part has to project enough to go around the pin to almost a complete circle as shown at left. In the suggested size, the length of a part will be about ⅝", but you might prefer to try wrapping a piece of scrap metal on the pin to get the length. In the best hinges, the bottom of the cut comes close to the pin and is beveled as shown at left (bottom).

Cut the two flat parts to fit into each other. Most sheet brass will bend to make a hinge without heat treatment but, if the brass is very hard, anneal it first. Use the rod that will make the pin for bending on. To make handling easier, leave it too long at this stage.

Hammer the projections from one side over the rod. It is helpful to have a creasing iron or a stake to support the work as shaping progresses as shown below (left) Closing the curve can be done with the end of a strip of metal used as a punch as shown below (right).

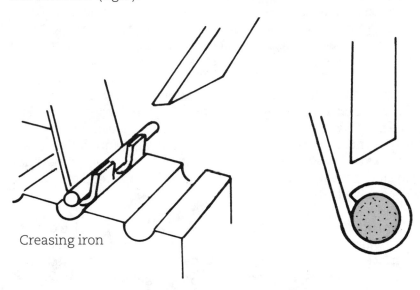

Creasing iron

Drive out the rod and do the same shaping on the parts of the second flap. Remove the pin and try the parts together. You will probably have to use a fine file to make the parts fit closely into each other.

Next, try the assembly on the rod to see if the hinge will open to a flat position. You might have to file more from the bottoms of the spaces.

Form a small rivet head on the pin and cut it to length so there is enough for a head at the other end as shown at right. Drive it through and form enough head at the other end to prevent it from coming out. Use a flat-ended punch to close in the curved parts.

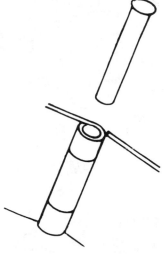

Hinges 51

Design considerations

The important consideration in the flaps of a hinge is the placement of holes for screws or rivets. An ornate hinge that is insecure will not fulfill its purpose, so the location of screw holes should come early in the laying out of a pattern. The flap of a very small hinge could have two holes, but three or more are usual in most hinge flaps. The holes need not be in a straight line, but it looks best to have them symmetrical. On short flaps, decoration is limited and has to be arranged around the screw holes as shown on page 49.

In most cases you can design the pattern by shaping the outline only, without bothering with cutouts. Be careful not to weaken the metal where it bends into the knuckle because that is where most of the load will come. Piercing in a small flap cannot be large. If there is a contrasting wood or other material to show through, however, piercing can be an effective decorative feature.

Sometimes one flap will be between edges, or otherwise out of sight, and it can be plain. Hinges that are to be mounted on the surface with flaps of equal size usually should have matching patterns both ways. Nevertheless, you might choose, for example, to use free-flowing leaf shapes that are complementary, but not the same.

Strap & T-hinges

It is in T- or strap hinges that you have more opportunity for decoration. Long straps can be the same both ways. T-hinges can have short flaps similar to those described for use when flaps are symmetrical. There have to be enough screw holes in both parts. Loads are greatest near the knuckle, so always arrange some screws close to knuckles.

T-hinges for boxes, cabinet doors, and other parts of moderate size can be made from brass or mild steel. You could use steel pins in brass hinges for extra strength, but for anything as heavy as a gate or a room door you should make the hinges of mild steel.

Manufactured T- and strap hinges have plain tapered pieces, often with the T-flap starting one part in from the ends of the knuckle. You can make hinges of this type with the shape softened by curves as shown below (top). A better hinge has the T-flap the full width of the knuckle as shown below (bottom). The greater width allows you more scope for decoration and you can pierce the metal, if you wish.

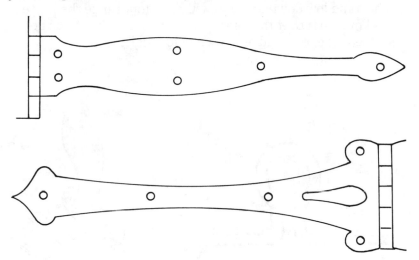

In some situations, such as on gate rails, long and narrow hinges look best, as shown below. Strength of fastening near the knuckle is obtained by arranging holes on each flap in a triangular form.

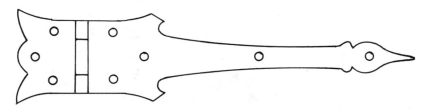

You are not limited to symmetrical patterns. You could draw a stylized leaf, which might then have a small leaf cutout, such as the one shown at right.

One advantage of making your own hinges is that they can be adapted to situations. You might have to allow for a part of a hinge, going through a molding, with a straight piece between shaped parts. You might have to raise the knuckle, as shown below left, to throw the swing of a door or lid clear of a surrounding molding or other obstruction. The break between lid and body of a box might come low down and you will have to arrange the hinge so its knuckle is over the joint and the long flap has to be bent over the angle of the lid as shown below right.

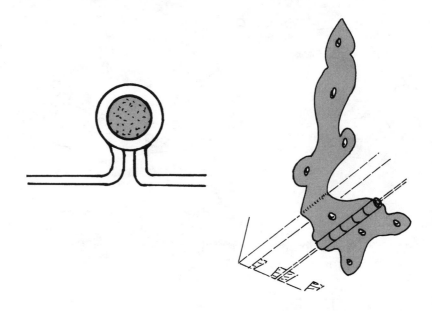

Box corners

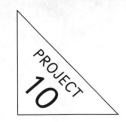

AT ONE TIME, most wood boxes and chests were reinforced by metal corners and strapping so they could stand up to rough use. Some of this metalwork was purely functional, but much of it was decorative. The family chest might have been the most important possession, and it was decorated accordingly.

Metal strengthening was necessary because woodworking construction methods did not produce very strong results. Today, with strong glues available and with modern power tools to cut joints, any wood assembly probably has enough strength in itself. Therefore, any added metalwork has to be regarded as mainly decorative.

You can add metal corners and other parts to a wood box (or other assembly) of any size. A large chest is the obvious choice, but a small box can be made very attractive with corners and other metal parts made in proportion. The corners could match hinges you make (see project 9). On a large chest, where strength is important, the corners should be mild steel. On a smaller chest or lidded box, they could be brass or copper. A polished hardwood box with polished metalwork can have a very luxurious appearance as shown at the top of the following page.

The design of box corners can range from fairly simple outlines to elaborate shapes with parts cut out. Whatever the final design, there are some basic considerations about the form in which you make the corners.

Design considerations

At most corners, you will want to cover the same amount each way—with similar decoration on each face as shown at bottom left of next page. The basic shape is a square as shown at bottom (center) of next page or circle as shown at bottom right of next page with a 90° cutout. The two cut edges then meet along a box edge.

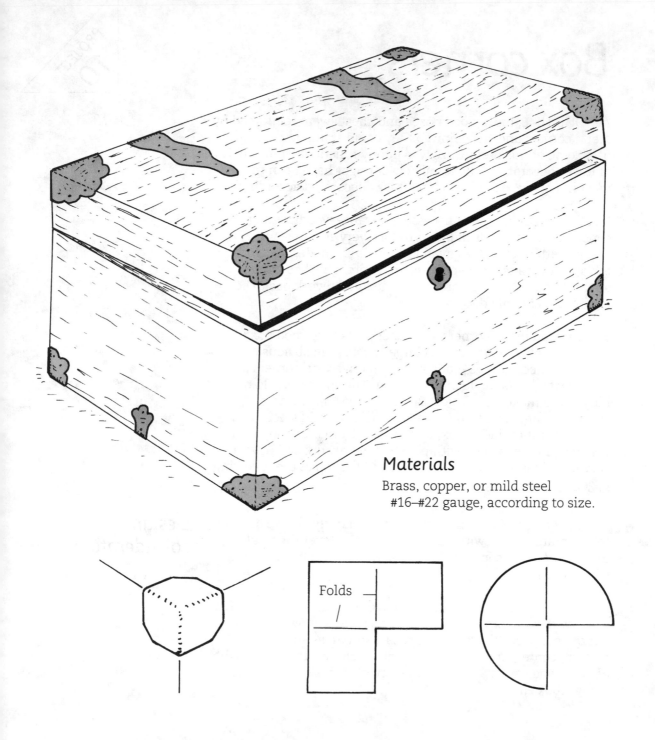

Materials

Brass, copper, or mild steel
#16–#22 gauge, according to size.

Folds

If it is important that the angle is covered, you can use a full circle or square with one cut and fold two parts over as shown below. Alternatively, you could allow a short flap to take one screw hole as shown at right.

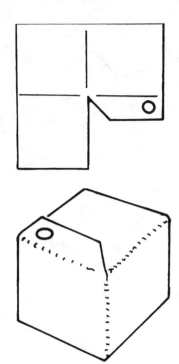

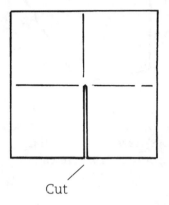

Cut

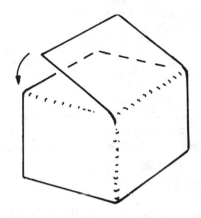

When the metal corner is at the bottom of the box, the lower surface will rarely be seen and you will not decorate it. In this case, you can cut the metal with two triangular pieces as shown below.

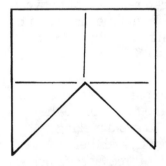

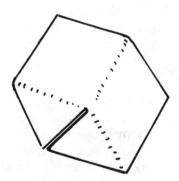

The amount of metal on each face does not have to be the same. On a shallow lid, you could allow for a large area on top, with shallower parts over the edges as shown at top left of the next page. If the box has a thick top and bottom boards, you might extend the overlapping metal parts to screw into the sides as shown at top right of the next page.

Your box corner designs have to allow for screws. Therefore, lay out enough hole positions to hold the metal flat. If you use

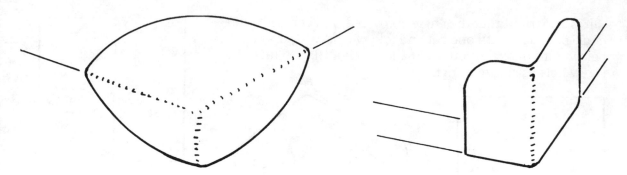

roundhead screws, they can become design features. If your
design would look best with screws less prominent, they can be
countersunk. Use slot-head screws; cross-head screws will not
present a traditional appearance. Use countersunk screws on
parts that will be under the box.

A large range of designs is possible and some are suggested on
the following page. Your choice of design might be affected by
the amount of repetition involved. You will have to repeat a
pattern several times, and you must not vary the shapes you
cut enough to be noticeable. At each corner you will repeat the
face design three times (although you can reduce that to two at
the bottom of a box). For a chest with lid, that means you will
have to produce faces of the metal to the same shape 18 or 24
times.

Getting started

You might wish to start by making a template of the design to
be used on one face. In any case, have the metal cut to the
basic overall sizes for all eight corners. To avoid making a
template, you can mark and cut one corner, and then use it to
mark another piece of metal on its two or three faces. When
you have cut that one out, you can use it as a template on the
others. Mark round with a fine-pointed scriber; with coarse
marking there is a tendency to mark and make subsequent
pieces larger.

The metal will be easier to hold for drilling if you make all
holes before shaping outlines and fretting openings. Be careful
with countersinking to get all screw heads finishing flush.

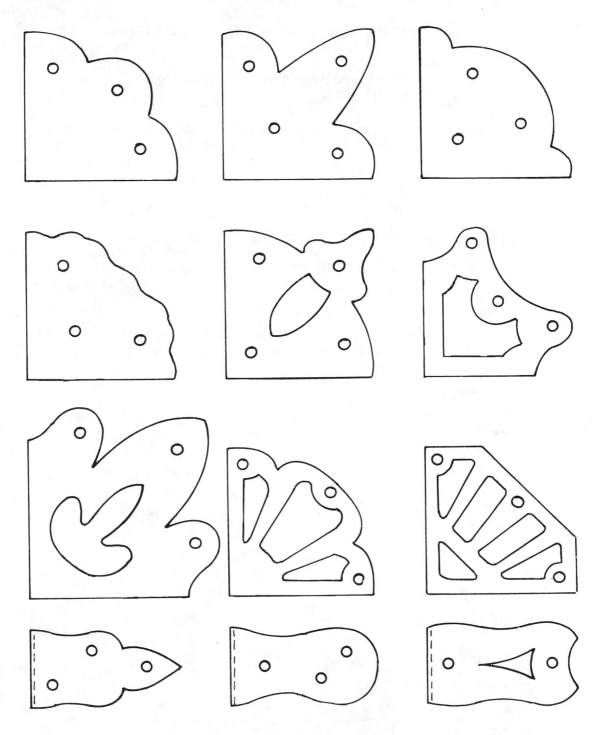

Straps, shown at the bottom of the last page, are not large enough for much shaping or piercing. If you decide to make some straps, make them to match the corners in the amount of overlap and the outline. You can also make hinges to match the set.

You can do the bending in a vise. Cover the teeth on the jaws with soft metal. Work at the ends of the jaws and use a hardwood pad between your hammer or mallet and the sheet metal. Check exactly the squareness of each bend as you make it.

Attaching the corners

When you fit the metal corners to a box, take sharpness off the angles of the wood that will come under the metal and round the wood corner. This will allow you to press the metal corner pieces tightly in place. Continue to press hard while driving screws.

If the outer corner of the metal finished sharp, hammer it to round it. If that is not enough, lightly file it. Be careful. Too much filing might go through to expose the wood.

Keyhole plates

A hole in wood for a key to pass through to enter a lock needs protection to prevent wear. A *keyhole plate,* or *escutcheon plate,* accomplishes this task, and even in poor light, it can help you place the key. A keyhole plate also provides you with a chance to decorate what might otherwise be a plain and uninteresting surface as shown on the following page. You can include the plate in the overall decorative scheme with matching corners and hinges on a chest (see projects 9 and 10).

The size of plate depends on the size of key. For something like a jewel case, the keyhole plate can be quite tiny and held with pins. At the other extreme would be the cover for a keyhole in a church door—made large and thick and held with several screws.

Most keys are of a shape that requires a round hole and a slot extending from it, usually downwards. If you need to match an unusual key, you can make the hole to suit without affecting the general design. You can fit a swinging cover to a keyhole plate to keep out dust and, in the case of a large keyhole, prevent anyone looking through from the other side.

Selecting your metal

Brass is the usual choice for a keyhole plate, though a very large one could be made of steel and finished by painting. You can use any other metal if you want to match other parts.

For very small plates your decoration will be in the shaping of the outline and the metal can be thin. A very small plate might be only #24 gauge, but #20 gauge will be stiffer. For large plates, you can choose between simply cutting an outline or adding further decoration by beveling. If you want to bevel, the metal should be at least $\frac{1}{16}$" thick; for outlines only, thinner sheet will be satisfactory on most keyhole plates.

Some traditional plates are very large and ornate with swirling outlines and many cutouts. If you are dealing with reproduction furniture, you might produce one of these plates.

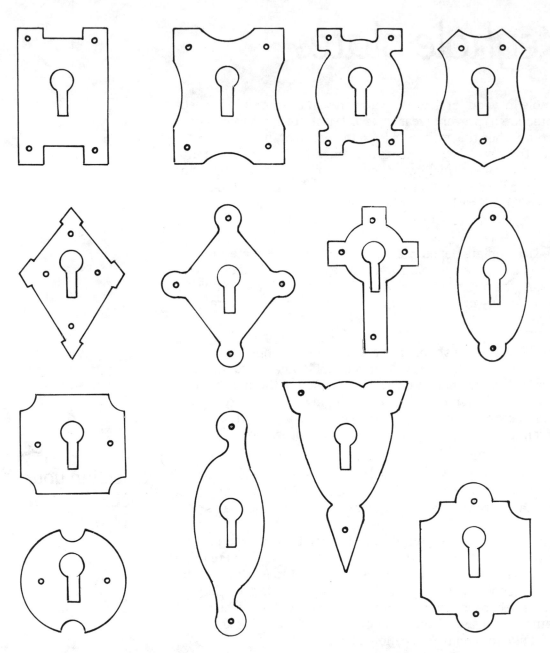

Materials

Brass or steel
#20–#24 gauge sheet metal or 1/16" thick (for beveling)

Otherwise, it is unusual to have decorative cutouts on a keyhole plate. In any case, choose your metal accordingly.

The most important part of the keyhole plate is, of course, the hole for the key. You should make this after marking out and before shaping the edges or other treatment. The hole has to allow you to enter the key easily, but you should not allow excessive clearance: One function of the plate is to guide the key towards the lock, and too much slackness will not do this.

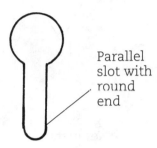

Parallel slot with round end

The keyhole can have a parallel slot with a round end, as shown at left, or the slot could be flared, as shown at right. A flared slot helps to direct the key in, even if the key does not have that section.

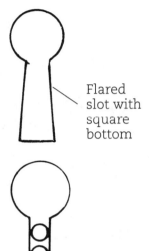

Flared slot with square bottom

Making the round hole is simple drilling. You can open the slot by drilling a series of holes as shown at right, and then breaking through with the edge of a file and trimming to shape. A slim *warding file*, as used by locksmiths, will do this work neatly. You also could use a fretsaw to cut the slot. Whatever method you use, see that edges finish smooth and that there is no roughness on either side.

Design possibilities

Although the number of patterns seems unlimited, you should decide on the basic form. Simplest is a rectangle as shown at right. A circle makes an interesting keyhole plate as shown at top left of the next page, although you might want to consider an ellipse as shown at the top of the next page (center). A diamond shape is also attractive as shown at top right of the next page.

Other shapes are mostly based on one or a combination of these outlines. The only exceptions might be the very ornate, traditional patterns or where you

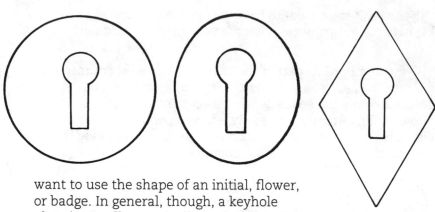

want to use the shape of an initial, flower, or badge. In general, though, a keyhole plate is usually too small in relation to the whole thing for unusual decoration to be very effective or to make much impact.

Some ideas for possible shapes are shown on page 62. All of these are intended to be cut to shape from thinner metal without bevels. Nonetheless, you should remove sharpness, particularly from front edges. Be especially careful that edges intended to be straight really are; errors will be obvious. There is more tolerance for slight errors on curves.

The size necessary to admit a key will determine other sizes. Leave enough space for holes. In most cases, you will get the best effect with roundhead screws. Use brass pins for the smallest plates.

Beveling

Using thicker metal and beveling gives a solid appearance. You could bevel all around to about half the thickness as shown at top left of the next page. Some of the patterns shown on page 62 could be used for thicker metal and could be beveled in this way. You can get an attractive effect by stopping the bevels, preferably with angled ends, so part of the outline retains square edges—the corners, in this case as shown at top right of the next page.

You can improve the appearance of a plate with straight outlines by making hollow bevels on some edges, as shown at the right on the next page, by careful work with a half-round file. On edges curved inward you can graduate bevels so they

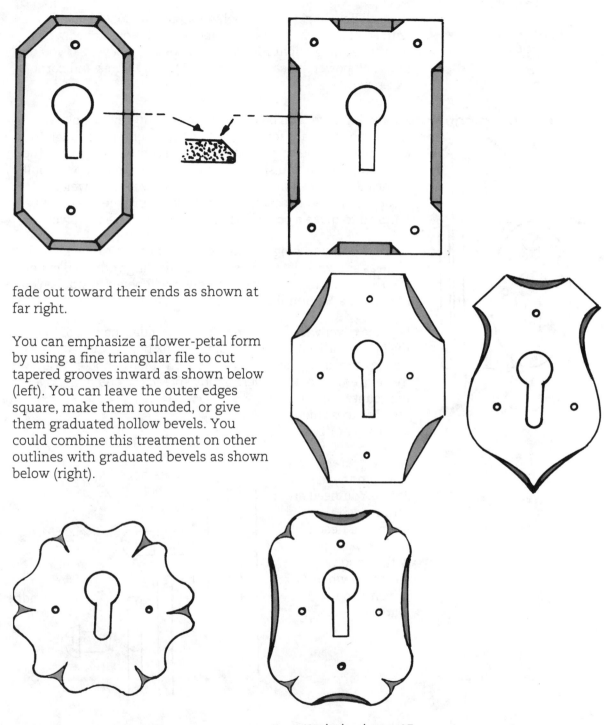

fade out toward their ends as shown at far right.

You can emphasize a flower-petal form by using a fine triangular file to cut tapered grooves inward as shown below (left). You can leave the outer edges square, make them rounded, or give them graduated hollow bevels. You could combine this treatment on other outlines with graduated bevels as shown below (right).

Keyhole plates 65

With all beveling, remove tool marks before polishing by hand with emery or other abrasive paper over flat or shaped wood. (Power-sanding might round angles and spoil bevels. If you do polish by power, be careful of wearing away edges and corners excessively.)

Fitting a cover

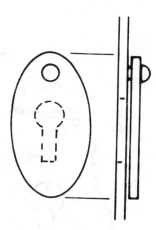

A swinging cover can be fitted to almost any keyhole plate. Allow enough space for the pivot and a cover large enough to go over the hole. The cover shape could be complementary to the plate outline, but you should keep it simple. Also keep the bulk of the metal low so the cover hangs shut by its own weight. Most patterns will accommodate these requirements; don't be tempted to make a cover with much metal above the pivot.

The cover must swing loosely and not too close to the keyhole plate as shown at left. Unless you are dealing with the keyhole for a lock on a massive door, the pivot will be quite small. You might use a ⅛" roundhead rivet.

Drill the cover with a clearance hole. Shoulder the end of the rivet to go through a smaller countersunk hole in the plate, keeping the unshouldered part of the rivet long enough to allow free movement of the cover. Lightly spread the end of the rivet in the countersink, and file off any excess metal as shown at right.

An alternative pivot is a roundhead screw. You need an unthreaded part under the head so the screw stops with enough clearance when driven into the plate.

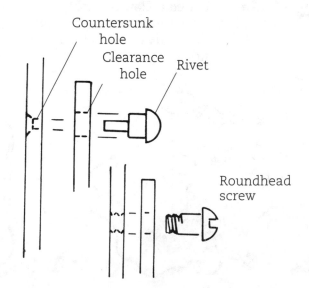

Countersunk hole

Clearance hole

Rivet

Roundhead screw

Plant container

PROJECT 12

A PLANT IN A PLAIN POT needs a container to give it a more decorative appearance. This container as shown on the following page is intended to be made from sheet mild steel, which could be #16 gauge or ¹⁄₁₆" thick. Galvanized or plated sheet will be protected from rust, but a painted finish on plain steel will serve the same purpose. For added protection, you could treat steel with rust inhibitor before painting.

This container as described, is intended to hold a potted plant. If you left out the cutout decorations in the sides and drilled a few drainage holes in the bottom, you could put soil directly into it. This would make it a useful ornament on your patio or deck, but you would have to use a tray to catch drips indoors.

Suggested size & design

The suggested size of the container will suit a plant in a plain pot of average size. It will provide a firm base for a considerable amount of foliage.

Of course, you could modify the sizes to suit your needs. If you alter them much, though, make sure the spread of feet is almost as much as the size of the top edge so your plant container will have enough stability.

In the design shown at the top of page 69, the corner joints are made by each side having one flap onto the next side as shown at bottom left of page 69. If you wish, you could alter this to flaps on both edges of opposite sides, with the other two sides plain. The shaped flaps are shown as decorative features on the outside, but, if you prefer, you could put plain flaps inside so only rivet heads show outside. The feet are bent so flaps at the top can take four rivets into the bottom of the container as shown at bottom right of page 69.

Making the container

Make the body of the container from one piece of sheet metal, with the sides folded on the base. On a piece of sheet metal at least 22" square, draw the two centerlines. Use the developed

Materials

Sheet mild steel #16 gauge or ¹⁄₁₆" thick
1 piece   22" × 22"
4 pieces   4" × 5"

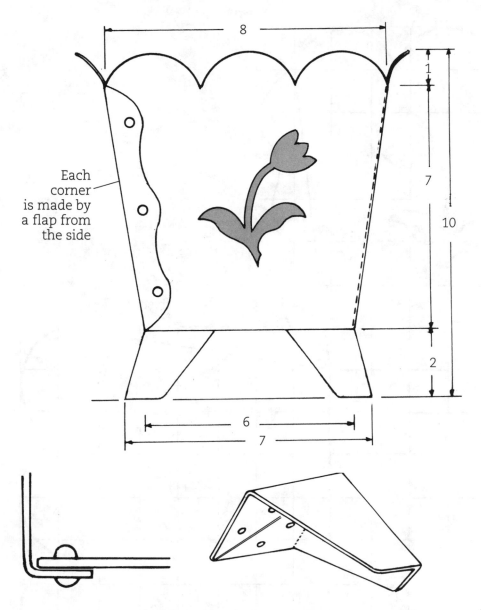

Each corner is made by a flap from the side

8

1

7

10

2

6

7

drawing on 1" squares to first mark the base as shown on page 70, and then draw four identical sides connected to it. Mark all fold lines, as shown.

Pierced decoration is not essential, but you might want to make a cutout pattern in one or all sides. The suggestion here is a

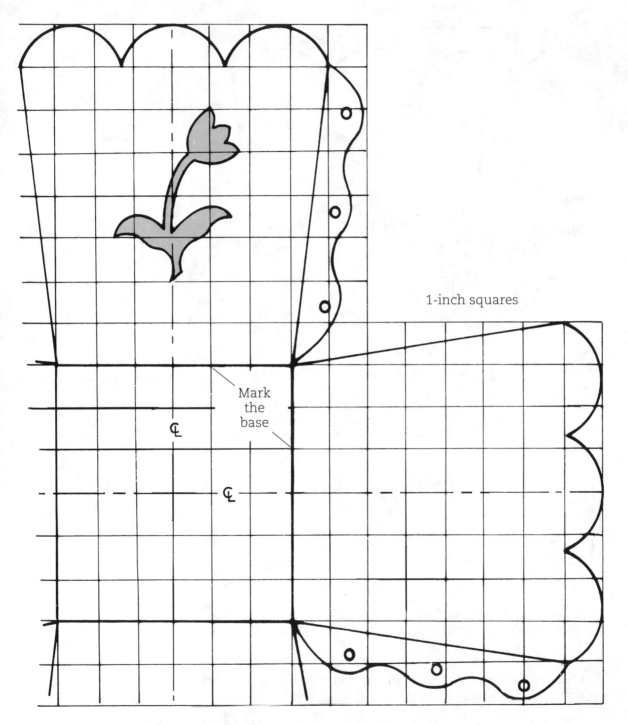

1-inch squares

Mark the base

C̵L

C̵L

flower as shown at the top of page 69, but you could cut anything from a simple initial to a complex badge or geometric form.

Complete all work on the edges before you do any bending. Smooth the edges, and round those that will be exposed. Drill the flaps for rivets $\frac{1}{8}$" or $\frac{5}{32}$". Roundhead rivets are the most likely choice, but countersunk rivets will also work well.

Partially bend all fold lines to ensure accurate positioning of the folds. Complete bending of the sides on the base so that the edges come under flaps. Make sure that the assembly is symmetrical and that the bottom has not been distorted.

Next, fold the flaps in turn over the plain edges, and clamp them together while drilling for top rivets. Close a top rivet at each corner; then remove the clamps and drill for the other rivets. At the top, you can have the manufactured rivet head outside and form the inside head by hammering. Because there is insufficient space to swing a hammer inside on the lower rivets, use the manufactured head inside, supported on a stout bar extending from a vise, and form the outside head with a hammer and a sett.

Flare the top edges outward by hammering the curved parts over a rod about 1½" diameter. The amount of curve is not as important as it is that all the parts match.

Cut the developed shapes of the four feet, and lightly round the bottom corners as shown on the next page. Drill the flaps for $\frac{1}{8}$" rivets. Mark the bend lines; then fold down the flaps and bend on the corner line so the flaps miter together as shown at the bottom right of page 69. Use the side view as shown at the top of page 69 as a guide to the angle to bend the flaps.

Drill the container base for the feet and rivet them on. Setting the tops of the feet a short distance in from the edges will be better than letting them project. Check that the container stands level and that there is no roughness on the bottom of the feet. Then finish all over with paint.

1" squares

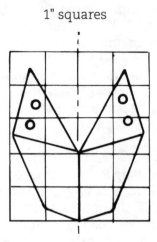

Trivet

IN THE DAYS WHEN food had to be heated over a fire in a grate, a stand was used in front of the fire at grate height so a pot could be slid onto it. The metal stand was called a *trivet,* because of its three legs, which were used because they would stand without wobbling on an uneven hearth. Few of us have need for a trivet in its usual purpose, but it makes a good plant stand, particularly if you have a plant whose foliage drops below the pot level. You could make a trivet to any height, but the one illustrated on the following two pages has a top 7" diameter supported 6" above the feet.

Because your trivet will almost certainly be used on a flat surface, you are probably not so concerned with preventing wobble, so you could fit four legs if you wish. The instructions provided here, though, are for the three-leg form.

Design and metal choices

If you so desire, the top could be mild steel. The trivet does not need to have a cutout, but you will probably want to decorate it with a pierced design, and that will look best in polished brass or copper. The supports here are made from ⅛" × ½" mild steel strip, which you might be able to bend cold, although you will be able to bend the top ring more easily at red heat over the beak of an anvil.

Making the parts

It will be advisable to start with the ring as shown on page 75. In this way, if it finishes a slightly different size than what you intended, you can modify other parts to match it. On a piece of metal, prominently draw a 6" diameter circle. You have to make the outside of the ring to fit this reasonably accurately.

Start with a strip at least 22" long, and hammer it progressively to match the circle, working from one end as shown at the top left of page 76. Continue until you have an overlapping full circle, and then cut the ends to meet. You might leave the ends free and depend on the top piece to hold the ring flat, but it would be better to join the meeting ends by welding or

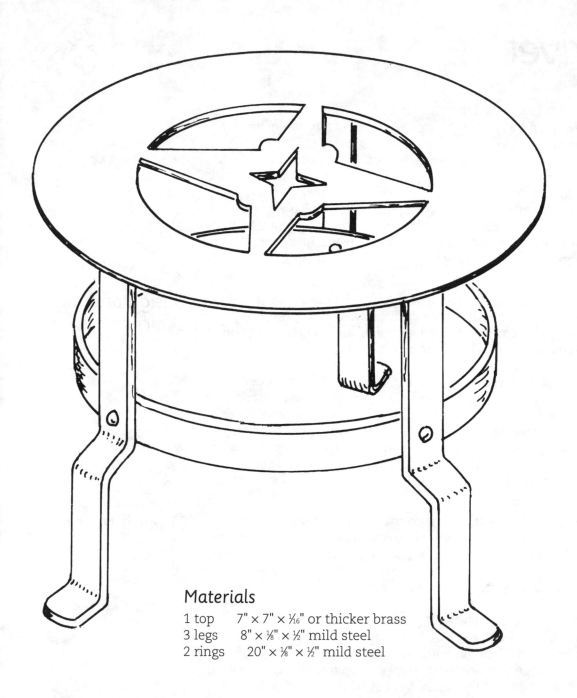

Materials
1 top   7" × 7" × 1⁄16" or thicker brass
3 legs   8" × 1⁄8" × 1⁄2" mild steel
2 rings   20" × 1⁄8" × 1⁄2" mild steel

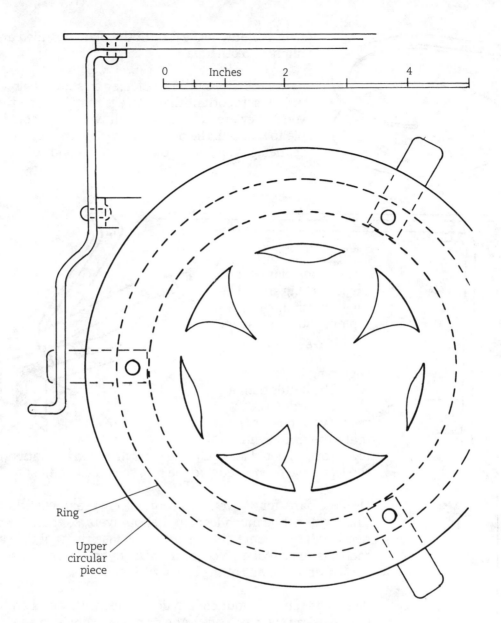

0   Inches   2   4

Ring

Upper
circular
piece

hard-soldering. Shape the complete ring to as true a circle as possible.

Cut the top circular piece, or plate, as shown above, 7" diameter (or 1" bigger than the ring you have made if you have altered the sizes). You could work a pierced design now, but you

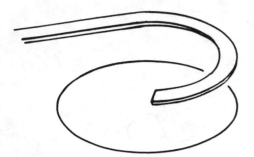

might prefer to leave it until the plate is drilled and matched to other parts.

Draw a full-size side view of a leg as shown below (left). It is important that the legs match each other, even if they are not exactly as drawn. You should be able to make all the bends in a vise without heating the metal as shown below. Round the ends of the feet (right).

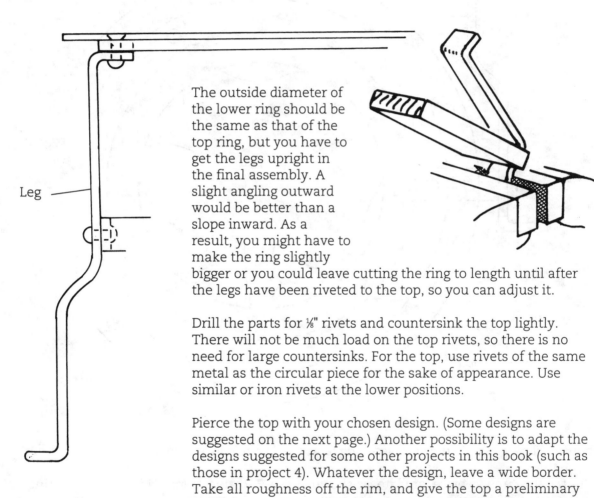

Leg

The outside diameter of the lower ring should be the same as that of the top ring, but you have to get the legs upright in the final assembly. A slight angling outward would be better than a slope inward. As a result, you might have to make the ring slightly bigger or you could leave cutting the ring to length until after the legs have been riveted to the top, so you can adjust it.

Drill the parts for ⅛" rivets and countersink the top lightly. There will not be much load on the top rivets, so there is no need for large countersinks. For the top, use rivets of the same metal as the circular piece for the sake of appearance. Use similar or iron rivets at the lower positions.

Pierce the top with your chosen design. (Some designs are suggested on the next page.) Another possibility is to adapt the designs suggested for some other projects in this book (such as those in project 4). Whatever the design, leave a wide border. Take all roughness off the rim, and give the top a preliminary polish.

Rivet the legs to the top and its ring. Adjust the legs, if necessary, so that they are square to the top or slightly angled outward. Try the lower ring in place, and adjust its size, if necessary. You could cut and weld or hard-solder the ends of this ring together. An alternative, which would have been the method used on original trivets, is to overlap the ends on a leg and rivet through as shown at the top left of the next page.

Assembly

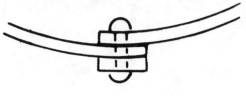

Traditional trivets had a handle for moving them away from the fire. If you want to follow this design, you can rivet a strip to one leg. For an all-metal handle, shape the strip into a grip, such as the one shown at left (center). You could make a wood handle by screwing on cheeks such as shown at left (bottom), or you could point the strip to go into a turned handle as shown below (right). Even if it is never needed for the original purpose, you might decide that a handle adds character.

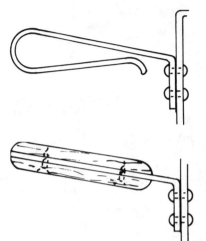

See that all rivets are tight and that the legs splay evenly, then remove any sharpness. The lower parts look best if they are finished with black paint; then the brass or copper top, with a high polish, makes an attractive contrast.

Letter or toast rack

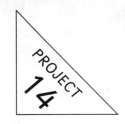

PROJECT
14

A RACK WITH SLOTS can have many uses. With it, you can keep envelopes and cards on a desk, you can sort letters awaiting reply, you can store sheet parts for model-making, or you can keep toast or slices of bread ready on a table, as shown on page 80.

A rack for workshop or hobby use can be made of any metal. Mild steel, in particular, would stand up well to shop wear. For letters and similar uses, brass, copper, or aluminum are suitable. For use with toast or other food, you will need to use a nonferrous metal, chromium-plated after making, or stainless steel.

Choosing the metal

If you use copper or brass for the racks shown on the following page, it should be at least #18-gauge thick. Some qualities are classed as *hard* or *half-hard*; if that is the case, you could use thinner "hard" quality. Aluminum should be slightly thicker. Most stainless steel is stiffer and you should be able to use #20 gauge.

This rack has six gaps, which should hold one slice of toast or a few letters each as shown at the top of page 81. Of course, you can vary the size and number of gaps to suit your needs. The basic rack is a single piece of sheet metal, which you can use as it is. (If you prefer, you could add a base, as described later.) The ends could be cut straight across or you can form lips for lifting as shown at the bottom of page 81. You can make better handles by extending and bending them as shown.

Set out the developed shape as shown on page 82, avoiding sharp angles as much as possible by rounding internally and externally. You could drill the corners of the slots to get uniform curves, then cut into the holes with a scroll saw or other tools. (If you will be fitting a base, be sure to drill before bending.) Smooth all edges. Make marking-out and bending

Making the rack

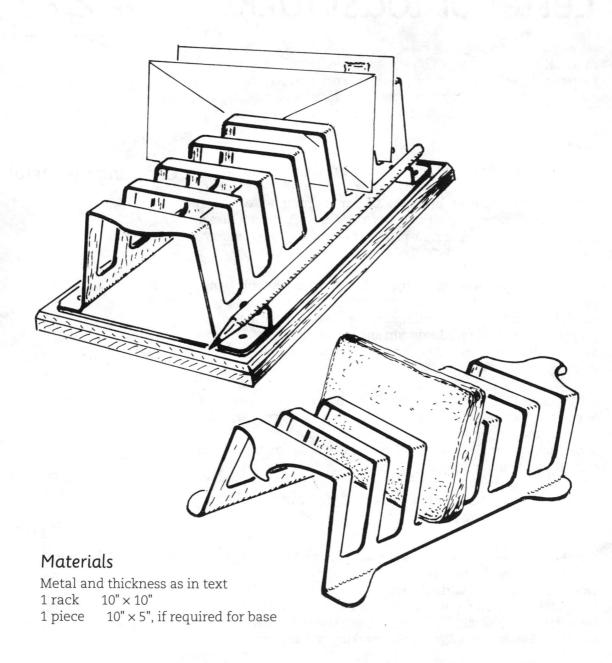

Materials

Metal and thickness as in text
1 rack   10" × 10"
1 piece   10" × 5", if required for base

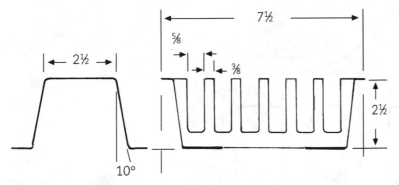

lines on what will be the inside surface. You might wish to polish the inside of the racks before bending.

Do not hammer directly on the metal. Instead, use a brake or bend the metal with a broad wood punch under the hammer. Let the sides splay out about 10°, and bend the feet so they are parallel with the top as shown at the top left of page 83. Sight along to ensure there is no twist. If you are using long handles, shape them next. Then feel for sharpness, which might develop on edges at bends, and remove it. Polish all over.

The rack as just described is complete and ready for use, but there are some possible variations.

Variations

Because this rack is light, you might wish to give it more stability, particularly if you plan to use it with papers on a desk. You could rivet a base of the same metal to the feet as shown above. The base can be up to ⅛" thick to produce weight, with either a straight or curved outline. Countersink the rivets

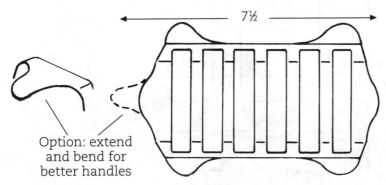

Option: extend and bend for better handles

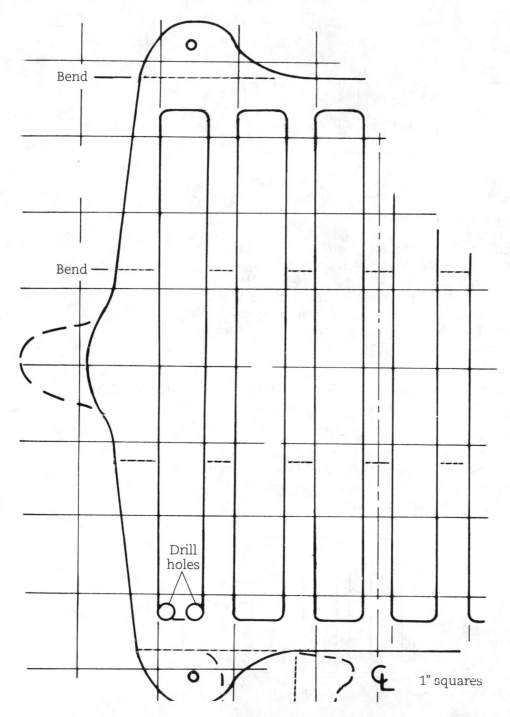

Bend

Bend

Drill
holes

CL

1" squares

82 Decorative Metalworking

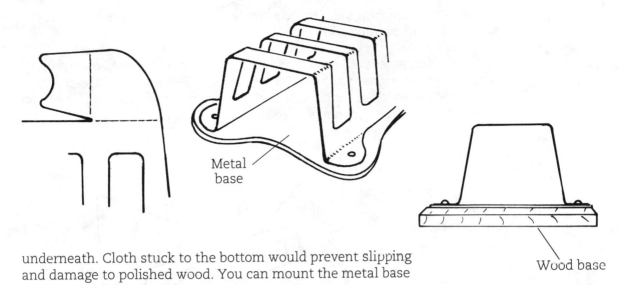

Metal
base

Wood base

underneath. Cloth stuck to the bottom would prevent slipping and damage to polished wood. You can mount the metal base on wood as shown at right.

If you have a lathe, you can turn feet and rivet them to the rack, either directly or onto bars put across the ends as shown below. This design is advantageous if you will use the rack for food. In such a case, the rack will have to be washed, and this more open way of

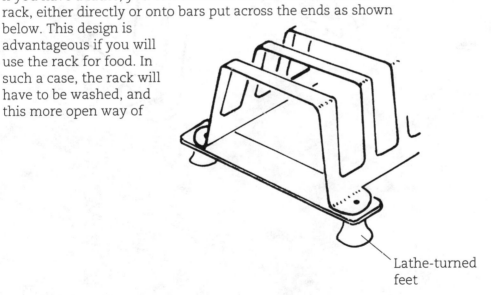

Lathe-turned
feet

increasing stability gives better access for cleaning than does an overall solid base.

A letter rack could have a place for a pen or pencil on one or both sides as shown below, by including suitable flaps on the developed shape as shown at the top left of page 83. If the rack is longer than a pen, you can arrange feet a short distance from the ends.

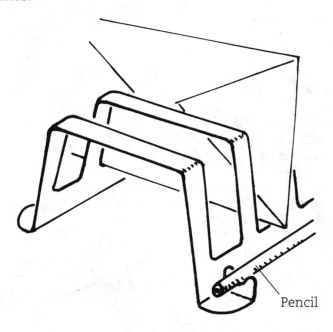

Pencil

Latch

ONE OF THE EASIEST WAYS to secure a door or gate is with a swinging latch in a notched catchplate on the gatepost or door frame. Ideally, such a latch will be on the side toward the way the door swings out. You might reach over a gate from the other side to lift the latch, but a better way is to have a lever through a slot in the door or gate. This can be combined with a handle for pushing or pulling the door. All parts could remain plain, but there is room for decoration on both sides of the door. This project is an example of how decoration can be done (see following page).

All parts are mild steel. You can either do some of the work by forging or you can build up and hard-solder or braze parts. You must allow for the thickness of the door, as that will affect the length of the lever. The size is not crucial, and the length suggested should suit doors between 1¼" and 2". If you want to make a small version for a small gate, remember the latch handle has to be gripped by a full-size hand.

The design suggested is a size to suit a normal door or a yard gate as shown at the top of page 87. The whole thing is in two parts. You make the latch and catchplate for one side of the door, then the lever and handle for the other side.

Start by making the lifting latch and the parts to go with it on the opening side of the door as shown at the bottom of page 87. All of the mild steel can be ⅛"-×-¾" strip.

Make the latch as shown at the bottom of page 87 with a hole for a ¼" rivet at one end and the other end shaped. You can make a curved outline as well. The latch is shown with a knob that serves not only as a handle, but also to add weight to help keep the latch down. You could forge a decorative shape with an end to be riveted into a countersunk hole with a large rivet or bolt. Although it is usual to fit a knob, it is not essential; you can lift the latch with the end of the lever.

Making the latch

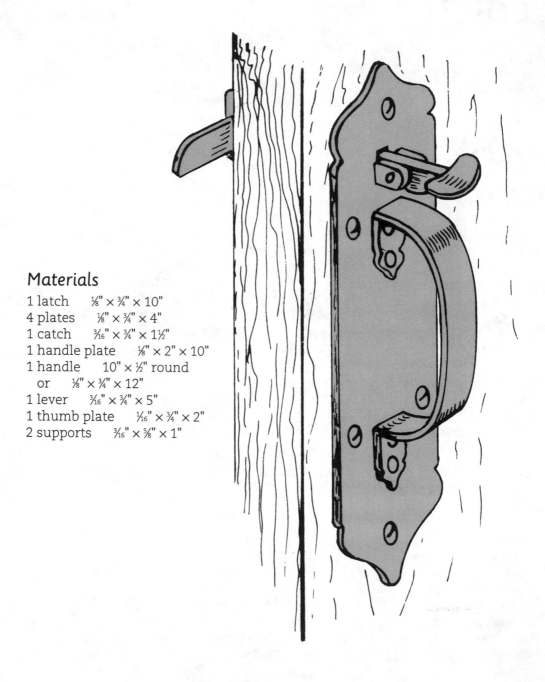

Materials

1 latch   ⅛" × ¾" × 10"
4 plates   ⅛" × ¾" × 4"
1 catch   ³⁄₁₆" × ¾" × 1½"
1 handle plate   ⅛" × 2" × 10"
1 handle   10" × ½" round
   or   ⅛" × ¾" × 12"
1 lever   ³⁄₁₆" × ¾" × 5"
1 thumb plate   ¹⁄₁₆" × ¾" × 2"
2 supports   ³⁄₁₆" × ⅝" × 1"

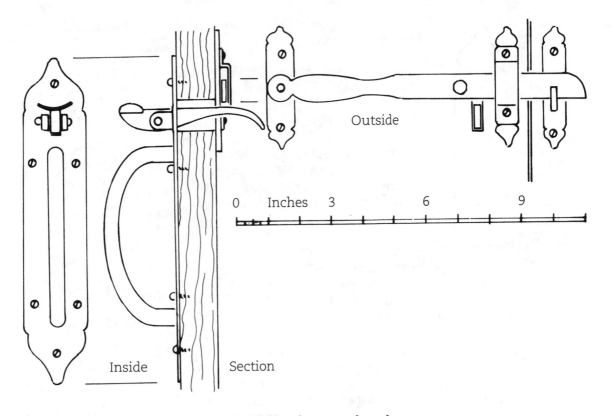

Outside

0 Inches 3 6 9

Inside   Section

To look right, the three backplates should be the same length and mounted in line. The part that might cause variations is the control plate as shown at top left of the next page. The arched piece has to clear the latch when the latch is in the down position. The same piece must have enough space above it for the latch to lift clear of the catchplate, with no excess

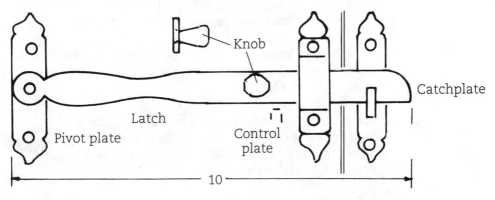

Knob

Catchplate

Latch

Pivot plate   Control
                     plate

10

Latch 87

clearance. A little over ¼" above the latch should be sufficient in most situations.

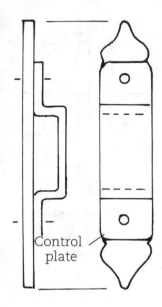

Control plate

Bend the arched piece, and mark and drill for ³⁄₁₆" diameter woodscrews. If this does not match the drawing, use it as a guide for marking holes in the backplate, which can be made to a suitable length and the other backplates cut to match.

Cut the pivot plate as shown at right with screw holes spaced the same as those in the control plate. Drill a central ³⁄₃₂" hole for the pivot rivet.

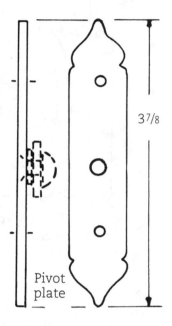

3⁷/8

Pivot plate

Cut the back for the catchplate as shown at top left of the next page, the same length as the others. Make the catch with a notch ⁵⁄₁₆" deep and with ample clearance for the latch. Shape the front in such a way that when the door is slammed, the latch will ride up over it. Cut a tenon to fit a slot in the backplate as shown at top right of the next page. File a countersunk back to the edges of the slot.

Assembling the latch parts

Shape the ends of the backplate so they all match as shown at bottom left of the next page, then prepare a pivot from a ¼" roundhead rivet as shown at bottom right of the next page. Reduce its end to fit the hole in its backplate, and arrange the part on which the latch pivots so it and a washer will move easily.

Rivet the pivot and the catch into their backplates. The control plate does not need rivets; the two parts will be held together by screws into the door.

You can make a trial assembly on the door or gate. Set backplates a short distance to each side of the door opening. When the latch is down, it and the ends of the backplates should be horizontal.

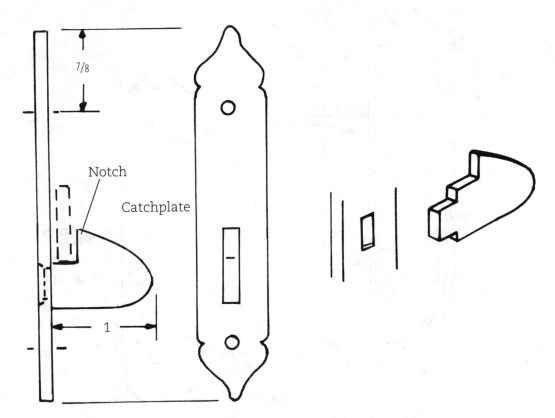

Notch

Catchplate

7/8

1

On the other side of the door, the handle and lever are attached to a large backplate that can be decorated to match the parts on the opposite side as shown at the top of page 90. The handle can be formed in several ways and the lever can be forged or fabricated.

Making the handle & lever

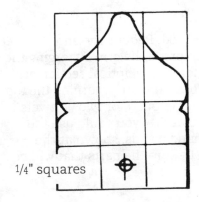

1/4" squares

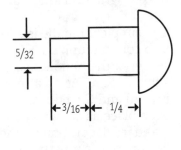

5/32

3/16   1/4

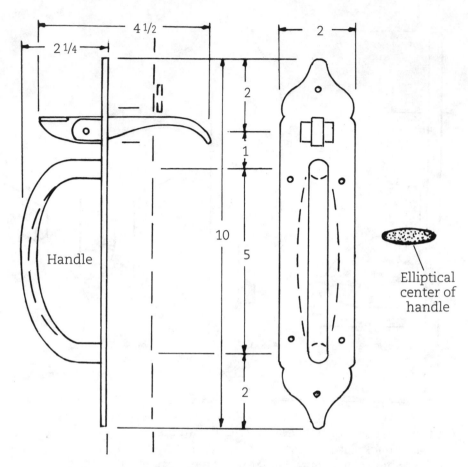

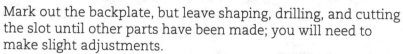

Elliptical
center of
handle

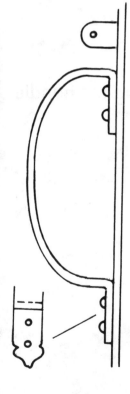

Mark out the backplate, but leave shaping, drilling, and cutting the slot until other parts have been made; you will need to make slight adjustments.

The simplest handle is a loop of ½" rod. Reduce the ends to rivet into countersunk hole. You can improve the grip by forging the center of the handle to a broad, shallow, elliptical section as shown above. As an alternative, bend flat strip, turning the top inward and the bottom outward far enough for two ³⁄₁₆" rivets at each place as shown at left. If you desire, you could use the standard decoration on the flat handle ends, shown at the bottom of the illustration at left. Be sure the parts that will be gripped are well-rounded.

Make the lever before you cut the slots or arrange the supports. To fabricate the lever, cut the outline shown below, and round the extending tail. Mark the hole, but leave drilling until you try the parts together.

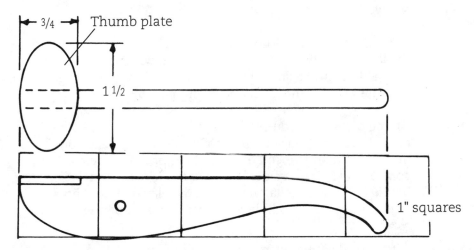

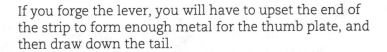

1" squares

Make the thumb plate round or elliptical, as shown, and round its edges. You could leave it flat, but it will be easier to use if it is hollowed as shown at right. Braze or hard-solder into the notched lever.

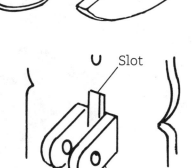

If you forge the lever, you will have to upset the end of the strip to form enough metal for the thumb plate, and then draw down the tail.

When you use the finished latch, your fingers will be around the handle and your thumb on the lever. The lever has to be located close to the handle, but there must be space for it to function. Cut the slot to allow easy side clearance for the lever. When horizontal, the lever should rest on the bottom of the slot. Cut the top of the slot high enough to allow movement as shown at right.

You could make tenons from the lever supports into the backplate, but it should be sufficient to braze or hard-solder them on the surface. Put a rod through the holes as an aid to accurate location while fixing. The holes are ³⁄₁₆" diameter and ½" from the plate.

Lever assembly

Next, try the lever in place. Drill its hole, and use a nut and bolt as a pivot, so you can take the lever out, if necessary.

Cut the backplate to shape and drill for woodscrews. Attach the handle to it. Leave out the lever until you have cut the door and screwed the parts on.

Cut a slot through the door that will give ample clearance to the lever and allow full movement. (You will probably find it advisable to drill a small pilot hole through first to check location.) Locate the latch and its support plates.

On the other side, you will have to arrange the handle far enough from the edge of the door to avoid knocking your hand, but the lever should come through the door fairly close to the control plate. Arrange the height of the lever so that it is nearly horizontal when the latch is down. The lever should lift the latch clear of the catchplate when the thumb plate is pressed.

Final finishing

After a trial assembly, remove the parts, round all exposed edges, and take off all sharpness. Paint all over, including the backs of plates to prevent rust. Paint the screw heads when you finally mount the latch pacts.

Display stand

FLOWER ARRANGERS usually like to have their displays shown at about eye-level and preferably on an isolated stand so there are no other things to distract from the beauty of the flowers and foliage. This might also apply to a prized object or a work of art you want to give prominence.

The stand shown on the following page is intended to support a single vase or other holder containing a large floral display at a convenient height. It is intended to be made of mild steel and finished with paint. If you can obtain a tube in metal other than steel, you may use that, with steel for the other parts. Obtain the tube first, though, as its size might affect the design of other parts.

This display stand is drawn as 1¼" square section with walls upwards of ⅟₁₆" thick. A size between 1" and 1½" would also be suitable. Sizes for the stand are suggested, but these could be varied to suit your needs or the available material, as shown at left on page 95.

Although it would be possible to join some parts with rivets, it is difficult to tighten them correctly in most positions, so screwed joints are suggested. These joints are all ¼" diameter, some using screws or bolts with nuts, and others with screwed rod between two nuts. In most cases, the rods pass through holes, but you need screw-tapping equipment in the plugs at the ends of the tube.

Cut the tube to length, and then file or machine the ends square to the sides. Make plugs 1½" long for the ends as shown at top right on page 95. Drill and thread central holes to take screws. You can fit the plug at the bottom as shown at bottom right on page 95, but leave the top plug out until after drilling other holes in the tube. You can shake out swarf from the holes before fitting that second plug in the same way. Once you have

Suggested sizes

Getting started

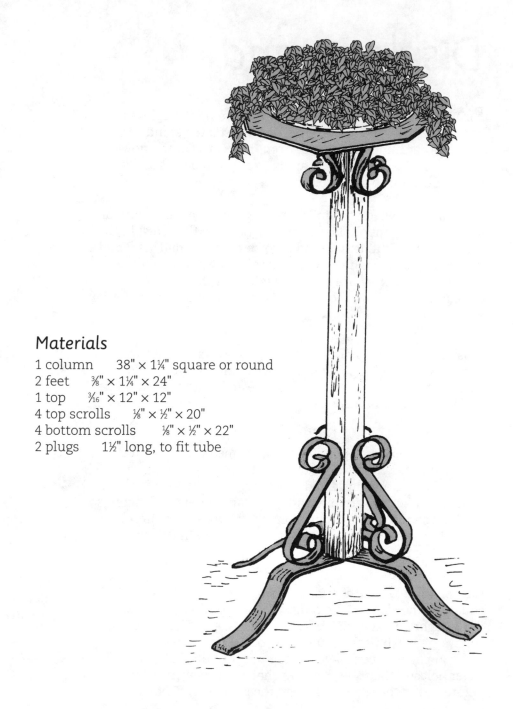

Materials

1 column   38" × 1¼" square or round
2 feet   ⅜" × 1¼" × 24"
1 top   ³⁄₁₆" × 12" × 12"
4 top scrolls   ⅛" × ½" × 20"
4 bottom scrolls   ⅛" × ½" × 22"
2 plugs   1½" long, to fit tube

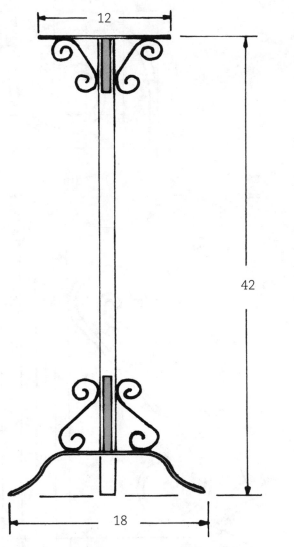

12

42

18

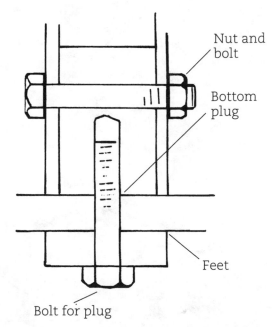

Top plug (don't fit in place until other holes are drilled).

Nut and bolt

Bottom plug

Feet

Bolt for plug

placed the bottom plug, drill across for a securing bolt and nut as shown.

The top is shown as octagonal, as seen at top left of the following page, but you could make it square or round. Edges are best rounded, but you should at least take sharpness off.

Display stand 95

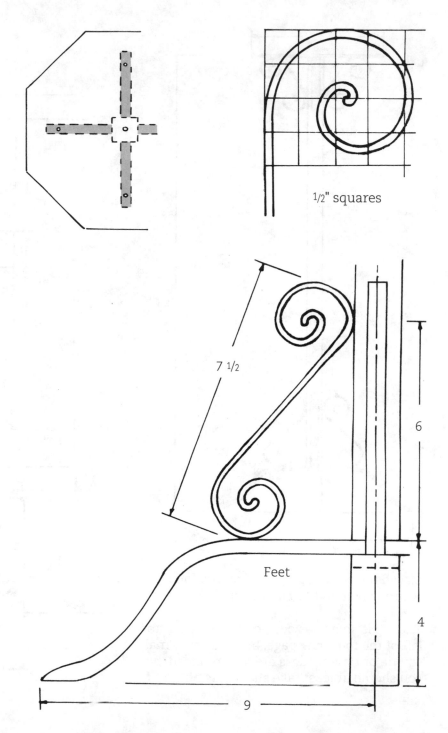

1/2" squares

7 1/2

Feet

6

4

9

96 Decorative Metalworking

The scrolls all have ends the same shape and size, as seen at top right of previous page, but the top ones have both ends curled outwards, while the bottom ones are reversed as shown at the bottom of the previous page.

If you already have a scroll iron for pulling strip around, you can use it, even if the result is slightly different from that shown; otherwise, standardize on the one shape shown. What is important is that each set of four match.

If possible, make the scrolls to the overall sizes shown. If yours are different, you can adapt the design to suit by altering the attachment points on the tube.

Making the scrolls

The feet cross under the bottom of the tube, as shown at the bottom of the illustration at the bottom of the previous page. This means you have to make them to slightly different curves so they will stand level on the floor.

Bend the ends of the upper foot, then bend the shallower curves of the lower one as shown below. Try crossing the feet on a flat surface, and adjust bends, if necessary, so they touch at the center. Drill the crossing for a bolt, and drive that into the tube plug as shown at the bottom right of page 95. Check that the tube is upright. If not, adjust the bends on the feet.

Making the feet

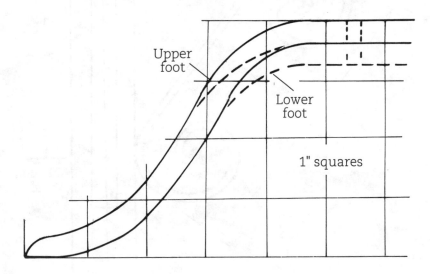

Upper foot

Lower foot

1" squares

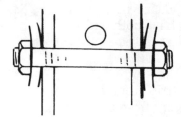

Try the bottom scrolls in position, using bolts downward into the feet. Use screwed rod (called *studding*) through the tube, and fit nuts at each end. Arrange the studding to cross at different levels as shown at left. The different levels of the crossing feet will allow for this.

Final assembly

Use a countersunk screw to join the top to its plug, and put the assembly temporarily in place to check the placement of the scrolls. Mark the position of the countersunk holes in the top for bolts when the scrolls are near 45° as shown below. So the crossing screwed rods miss each other, arrange them far enough above and below the measured position on the tube.

Shake out swarf, and then secure the top plug and join all parts. Remove any sharp edges, and finish all over with paint.

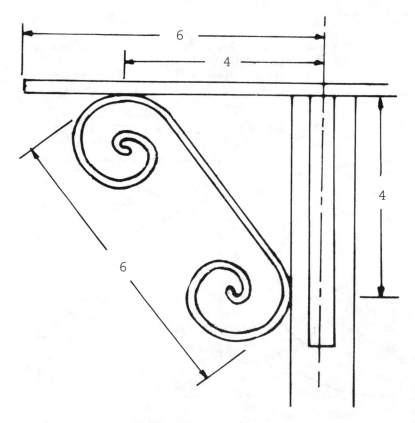

Tankard & jug

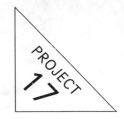

A TANKARD AND TRADITIONAL JUG or pitcher both have handles and can be made with the same basic bodies as shown below. They can be made of brass, copper, gilding metal, or a combination of these. A jug is particularly attractive if its lip is made of copper and its body of one of the other metals.

If you intend to use these containers for drinks, you should make them silver- or chromium-plated. In their natural states, this tankard and jug can be used as a decoration in themselves, or as containers for flowers or plants.

Materials
1 body   6" × 14" × #18 gauge
1 bottom   4" × 4" × #20 gauge
1 bottom   ⅛" × ⅛" × 15"
1 handle   1⅛" × 9" × #20 gauge
1 jug lip   5" × 9" × #18 gauge

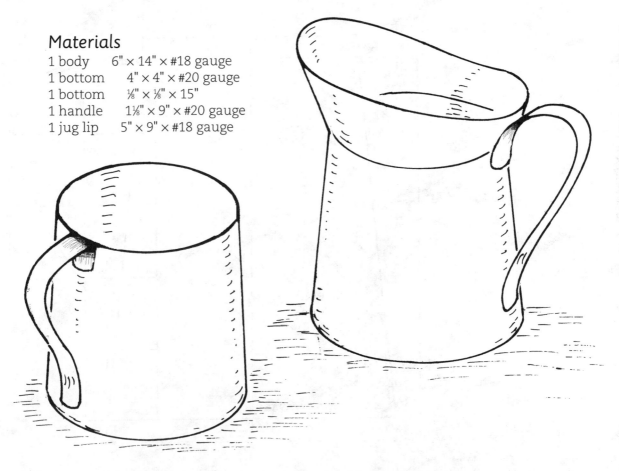

The basic body is best made of fairly thick metal, not less than #18 gauge. The jug lip could be the same or thinner metal. Handles have folded edges and could be #20 gauge or thinner.

Making the tankard

To make a tankard, first set out a full-size side view, such as the one shown below, and develop the shape. (You can do this as shown in project 8, at the top of page 45, with an improvised compass.) If you extend the sides of your drawing, they will meet at about 19". An alternative, particularly if you decide on a shape with less taper—and, therefore, a potentially longer radius—is to make a paper template of the side view and use this to repeat a total of about 3¼ views as shown at top left of the next page, drawing curves through the meeting corners. This should produce a similar result to using a compass.

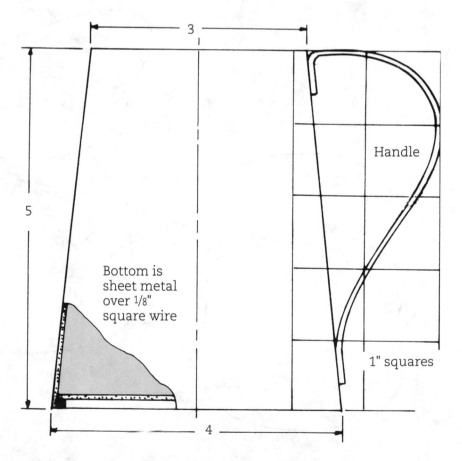

3

5

Bottom is
sheet metal
over 1/8"
square wire

Handle

1" squares

4

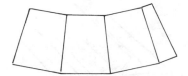

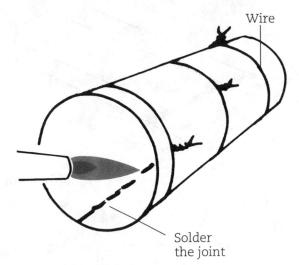
Wire

Cut the developed outline, and roll it to shape. File the meeting edges slightly hollow inside. Tie with soft iron wire, and join the edges with hard solder, as shown at right. Scrape off any surplus solder inside and out, and true the shape.

Solder the joint

Planish all over. You could use a hammer with a slightly curved face to get an almost smooth effect. If you prefer a pronounced dimpled appearance, use a hammer with a more domed face. Level both ends of the tube, and round the top edge.

The bottom

The bottom is a circle of sheet metal over a ring made from ⅛" square wire as shown on previous page. File the meeting ends slightly open as shown at right, and braze or hard-solder them together. You could make the ring slightly too small and hammer it over the beak of an anvil until it stretches to fit. However, if you make it too big, all you can do is cut something out and join the ends again.

Make the circle of sheet metal to fit above the ring, and soft-solder these parts in place. You will probably find it best to have the tankard inverted. Apply flux and heat gently with a flame until you can touch the end of a stick of solder on the joint and it will melt and flow around. Then scour the tankard clean with pumice or other powder, and wash and dry it.

The handle

The handle could be solid metal, but folded sheet metal is light and forms a comfortable grip. Mark sufficient length with bend lines as shown at top left of the next page. Square-edged metal ¾" wide will help you start the bends accurately as shown at top right of the next page. Most sheet metal will bend satisfactorily

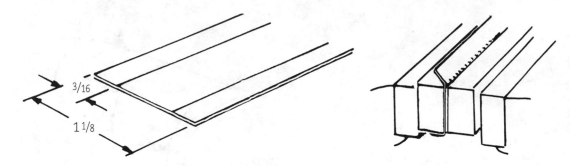

in the state it is supplied, but if it is hard, anneal it before bending.

Close the bends by using a piece of wood as a punch, as shown at left. Leave a section with evenly curved edges.

Bend the handle to shape, with the folds inward, using the illustration on page 100 as a guide. Round the ends, and hollow them to conform to the curves of the tankard. It is a help in making the joints if you coat the joint areas of the handle with soft solder. Have the tankard surface clean, and coat the joint area with flux. Wire on the handle, and make the joints with no more heat than necessary to make the solder flow. Too much heat would remove the hardness given by planishing and it might melt the solder holding the base. (If you can obtain soft solders with different melting points, you can use the soft solder with the lower melting point for the second joints.)

Finishing   Except for removing any excess solder and polishing all over, that completes the making of a tankard.

Making the jug

Making a jug is different than making a tankard. The latter needs to have a lip or a spout and it could curve higher as shown on the following page. The body and base are the same as the tankard, though, and you can modify sizes if you wish. (A taller jug might be better if you plan to use it for holding flowers.)

Make the body in the same way as for a tankard, but do not round the top edge.

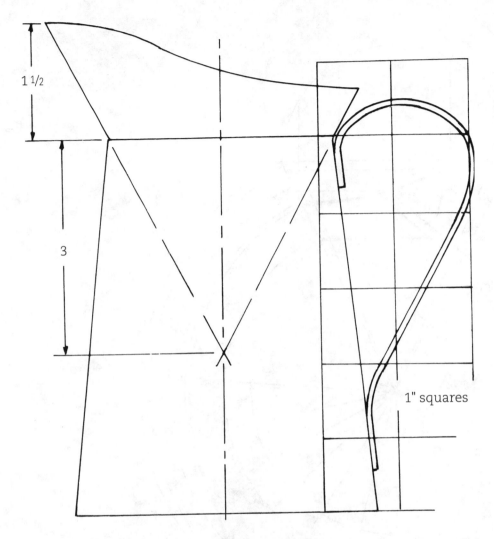

1 1/2

3

1" squares

Getting the shape for the lip is an interesting problem in development. The lip slopes outward evenly all around so it is part of a cone, but its edge is curved to give a pleasing shape and to form a spout for pouring. Opposite sides of the lip are the same, so you only need develop half and turn that over. Arrange the joint at the narrowest part.

Following the top portion of the illustration on page 104, draw a full-size side view of the lip and complete the cone by continuing to a point and drawing a line across the highest

Creating the lip

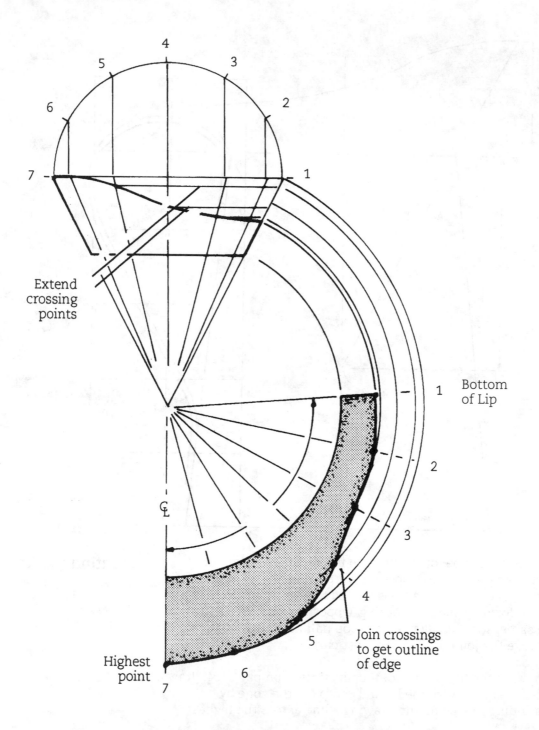

Extend
crossing
points

Bottom
of Lip

Join crossings
to get outline
of edge

Highest
point

104 Decorative Metalworking

part. Draw a semicircle on the base, then divide the semicircle into six parts of equal size around the circumference. Project straight down from these points to the base of the cone, then to its point. It is where these diagonal lines cross the shaped outline that is important. Project the crossing points to the side of the drawing to complete the preparation of the side view.

Turn your attention now to the bottom half of the illustration on page 104, and draw a development of half the cone. Follow round radii of the bottom of the lip and its highest point. The distance around the circumference of the bottom of the lip should be 3½ its diameter. You only need half that to measure around from the centerline. Leave a little extra at the narrow part for final adjustment.

Once again, divide the development into six equal spaces with radiating lines. It will help to avoid confusion if you number the points on both parts of the drawing. The lower edge of the lip is a smooth curve, but you have to get points on the radiating lines to mark the developed shape of the outline of the top edge. Project these around from the side drawing. Join the marked crossings to get the outline of the edge. Make a template from this half-drawing, and use it to mark the metal. Cut it, and roll it to shape.

Adjust the size of the lip so it will press into the top of the body. You can file the inside of the top of the body to match the slope of the lip as shown below. Also, you could flare the lip a little by hammering it over a stake before filing. This will give a wider surface for soldering as shown at far right. Cut and join the meeting ends of the lip. You could planish the lip or leave it plain.

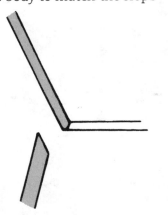
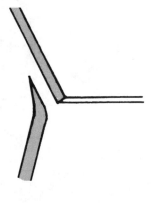

Assembly & final steps

Fit the lip into the top of the body and soft-solder it there. If you can apply pressure with weights or clamps, you can ensure a close fit. Trim the inner edge of the lip close to the inside of the body as shown at right. Of course, if the jug will only be used for flowers, it will not matter if the lip projects inside.

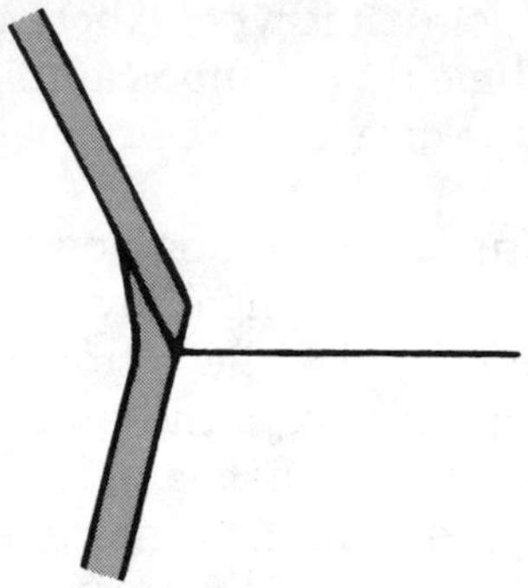

The handle could be the same as on the tankard, but it will look better if it is looped higher. Except for the different shape you can make it in the same way.

Shelf brackets

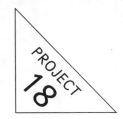

THE SIMPLEST SUPPORT FOR A SHELF is an angle bracket
made of metal that is stiff enough to resist bending under load.
A better bracket has a diagonal strut to help share the load. It is
possible to use this basic form to develop decorative designs as
shown below.

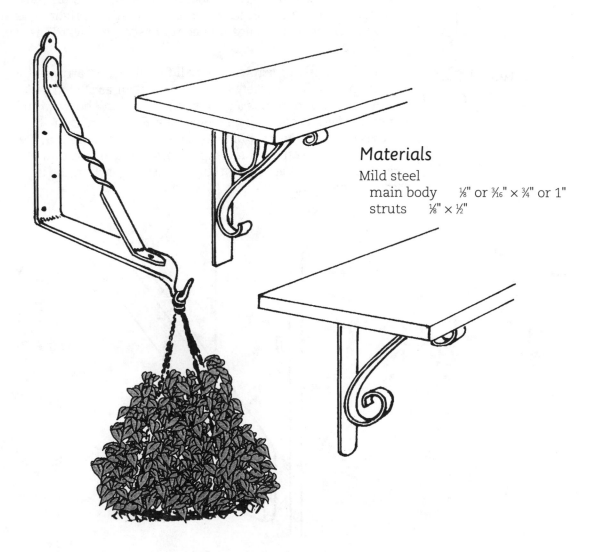

Materials
Mild steel
  main body   ⅛" or ³⁄₁₆" × ¾" or 1"
  struts   ⅛" × ½"

The wall load on a shelf bracket comes mostly on screws near the top of the upright leg. Therefore, there should be more screws near the top than there are farther down. The standard is to have two screws, arranged diagonally, at the top with one screw at the bottom, as shown at left.

In a larger bracket, you might need to use more screws. In this case, you can arrange screws upward into the shelf in any convenient manner, as there will be less load on them. If you invert a bracket to support a shelf from above or to take a hanging lamp or flower basket, the load on the upright leg is reversed, and you will again need more screws toward the top.

Bracket size & design

For ease in driving screws, you will find it best to arrange the main part of the bracket wider than its strut as shown below. You do not want to risk a shelf sloping forward, but it would not matter if it had a slight slope back. For this reason, it is advisable to make your bracket a degree or so more than 90°. Because of the effect of leverage, a bracket will resist its tilting load better if the leg against the wall is longer than the leg under the shelf.

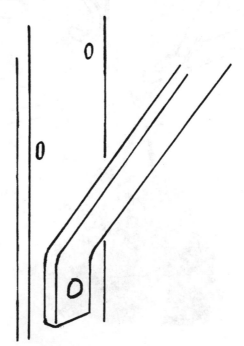

You can use many sections of mild steel, but in the examples it is assumed that the brackets are of moderate size and that the main parts are ⅛" or 3⁄16" × ¾" or 1", and that the struts or scrolls are ⅛" × ½".

The illustration shown below (left) is a simple strutted bracket. You could add decoration by heating and flattening ends and filing the outlines, as shown in the illustration below (center) or you could roll them, as shown below (right).

Design possibilities

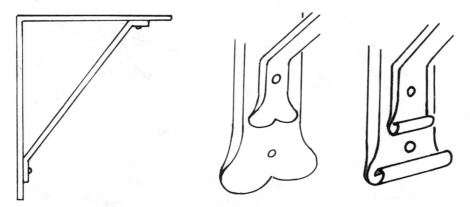

You could give the strut two twists by heating its center and twisting it as shown below.

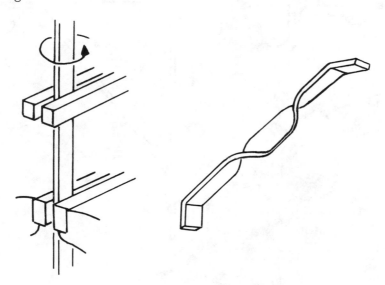

If the heat is even, you will get a regular twist, such as the one shown below (left). If the heat is hotter at the center, you get a twist that is tighter in the center as shown below (right).

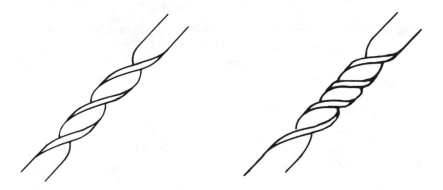

The end of a shelf bracket can have a hook for hanging a variety of things indoors or outdoors as shown below (left). You could simply bend the full-width strip, or you could heat it and forge it round. Another possibility is to do this at the end of a strut, as shown below (right), repeating at the bottom for decoration.

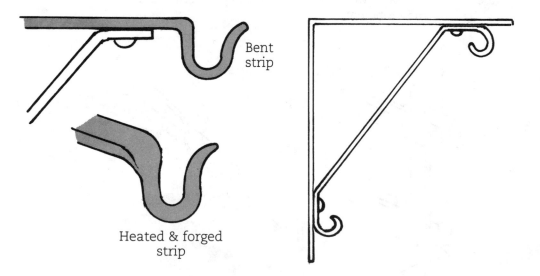

Bent strip

Heated & forged strip

The scroll design is a versatile one, and there are many variations of it as shown below. An effective way to use a scroll design for your bracket is to use it in place of a strut, using equal or unequal twists.

If there are two parts to be joined, you might be able to drill and bolt through. More likely, though, the pattern you use will involve parts that get in the way of drilling. The blacksmith's method of joining is to use a *clip* as shown at right, which is a piece of thin strip closely wrapped around. Prepare it open as shown at right (bottom) so it can be slipped over, then squeezed tight with a clamp or hand vise. The illustrations shown below are examples of clips in use.

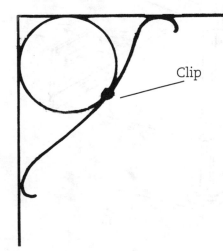 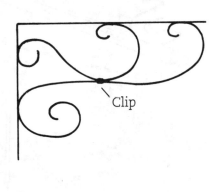

Clip

Clip

Shelf brackets 111

Weather vane

NOT ONLY DO WEATHER VANES tell the direction of the wind, but they also make a decorative addition to the top of a building. The example shown below incorporates a rooster, or *cockerel*, which is a common figure in weather vanes and which justifies the frequently used name of *weathercock*.

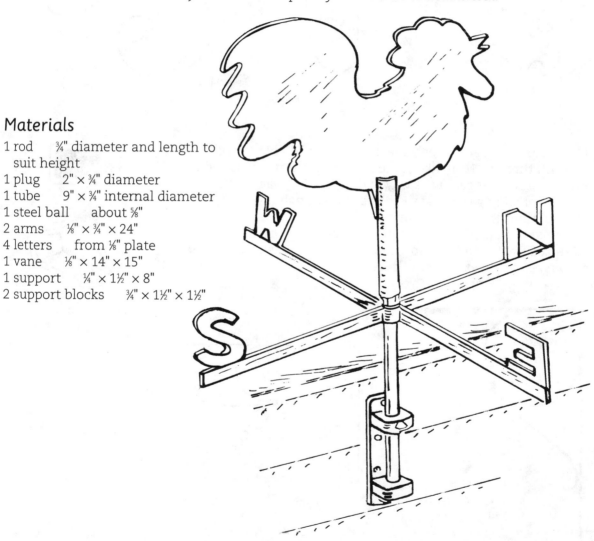

Materials

1 rod   ¾" diameter and length to suit height
1 plug   2" × ¾" diameter
1 tube   9" × ¾" internal diameter
1 steel ball   about ⅝"
2 arms   ⅛" × ¾" × 24"
4 letters   from ⅛" plate
1 vane   ⅛" × 14" × 15"
1 support   ¼" × 1½" × 8"
2 support blocks   ¾" × 1½" × 1½"

The size suggested as shown on page 114 is suitable for mounting on a garage or shed, or on a pole in a yard. If you want to make a weather vane to go at the top of a tall house or at a similar height above the ground, you must make it bigger so that it has enough visibility.

The device only performs its function fully if it is mounted where it can be affected by the wind coming from any direction. Otherwise, it might be decorative, but it would not be a practical wind-direction indicator.

If you do not want to use the cockerel for the weather vane, feel free to use almost any pattern you choose. The only requirement is that the pattern must have its largest part on the side of the pivot point toward the direction the wind is blowing. In other words, for the vane to work in a light wind, the area on that side must be appreciably more than on the other side of the pivot. Some suggestions to solve the problem: A single arrow could have large "feathers," or your chosen device could be placed only on that end.

Suggested size & design

Construction should be with mild steel. The main support is a ¾" round rod, and you will need a piece of stout tube to fit over this and rotate freely.

The pivot is a steel ball that fits easily in the tube. If the tube is then packed with thick grease, the weather vane should work for a very long time without attention.

The method you use to support the main rod will depend on your particular situation, but the instructions allow for attaching to a wall. It would be advantageous if you can weld some parts, but alternative constructions are suggested.

Construction

Prepare the upright assembly first. The tube length suggested allows about 4" overlap on the rod as shown on page 115. That should be sufficient, but you could make more of an overlap if you deem it necessary. Prepare a rod of sufficient length, and level its ends. Cut the tube to size, and make a slot in the top to suit the steel plate to be used for the vane. Make a plug to go below it, and fix the plug in with a rivet. You can either weld

Making the weather vane

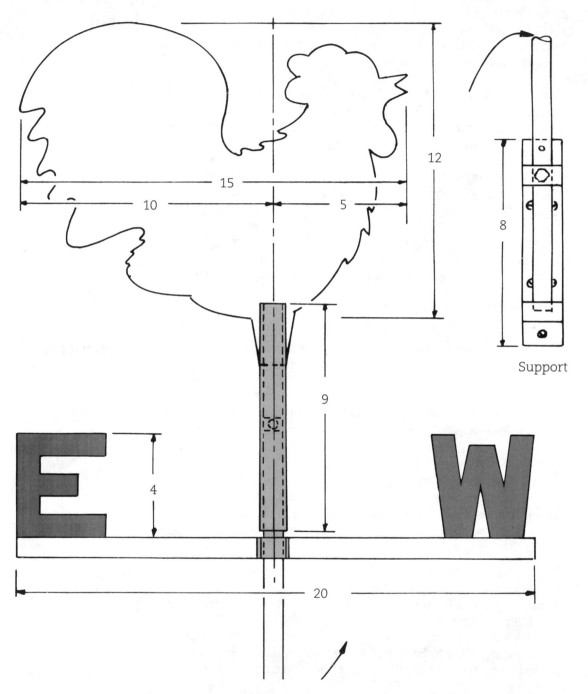

15

10

5

12

9

8

Support

E

W

4

20

114 Decorative Metalworking

the vane into the slot or drill for rivets (use ³⁄₁₆" rivets throughout).

Cut the vane to shape following the illustration grid shown on page 116. Small variations in detail will not matter, but you should try to get the main outlines correct. Once you have cut out the outline, remove roughness. Next, fit and weld or rivet the vane into the tube. If you desire, fill the spaces in the tube each side of the vane with flexible stopping to prevent the accumulation of rainwater there.

The arms to carry the letters are ⅛" thick. For the size suggested, it should be sufficient to use ¾"-wide strip, but you could use stouter metal. This is particularly important if you increase the suggested size. Bend the centers of the strips to fit against the rod as shown at right on page 117.

The letters indicating compass directions should be plain and bold so they are easy to identify from a distance as shown at the bottom of page 117. You could weld them on top of the arms or include extensions so they can be riveted through the sides. Attach the arms to the rod ¼" below where the bottom of the tube will come. You could use a nut and bolt or a rivet as shown at right on page 117.

The recommended method for mounting the assembly is by attaching it to a wall using a backplate that is ¼" × 1½" × 8" as shown on page 118, with two blocks that are ¾" thick. The top block has a hole through to take the rod, and you can drill the bottom block halfway to provide a support. If you have the facilities, weld these parts together. An alternative is use screws. Drill the backplate for sufficient fixing woodscrews.

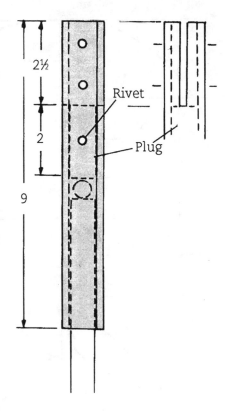

Mounting the assembly

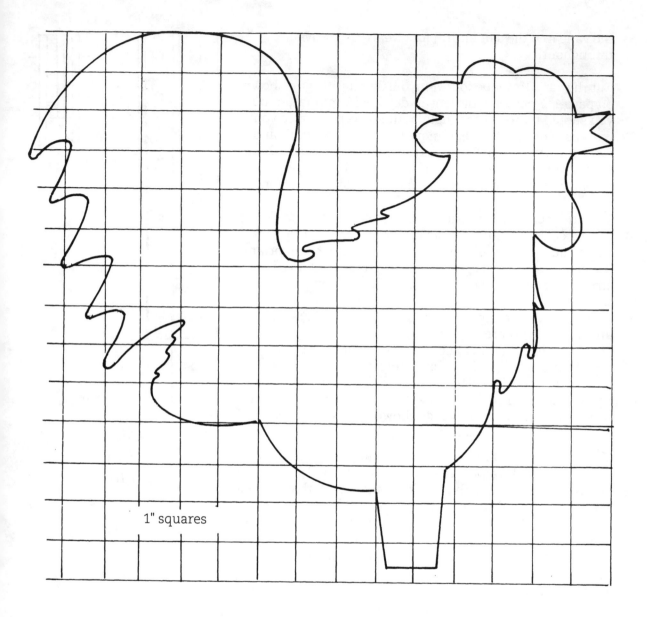

1" squares

When you mount the weather vane, you will need to rotate the assembly with the aid of a compass to get the arms correctly oriented. (Be sure to keep the compass far enough away so its needle will not be deflected by the steel.) Lock the rod in position with a screw. Make the rod long enough to put the arms and operating parts far enough above the roof or other obstructions to the wind.

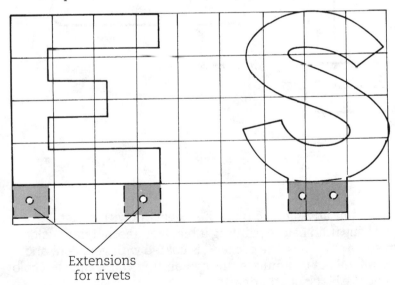

Attach with nut and bolt or rivet

10

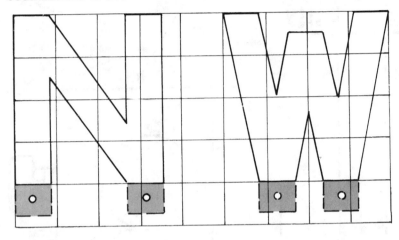

1" squares

Extensions for rivets

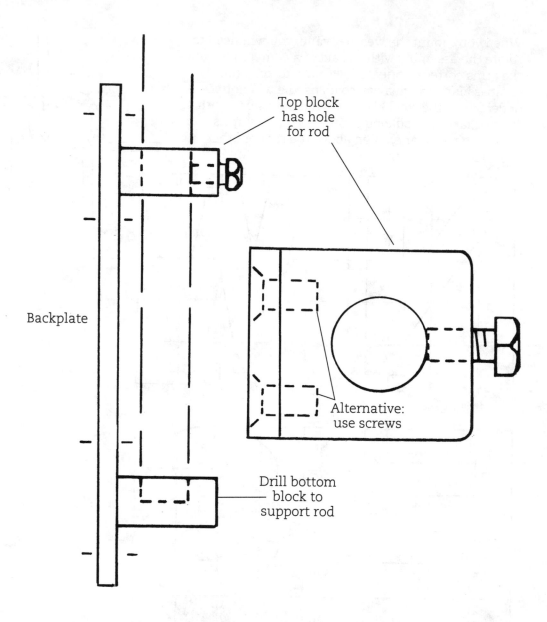

Top block
has hole
for rod

Backplate

Alternative:
use screws

Drill bottom
block to
support rod

It would be advisable to treat the steelwork with a rust-inhibiting fluid before painting it black or another dark color. On some churches, the cockerel is coated with gold leaf, and you might like to simulate this by painting yours a golden color above the black of other parts.

Letter openers

YOU CAN MAKE LETTER OPENERS from hard brass or combinations of steel and other metals. Although knifelike, a letter opener does not have to cut anything tougher than paper, and it does that by tearing. For these reasons, it does not need the fine cutting edge and hardness of tool steel.

You can use your own ideas for patterns, but the important considerations are a part to grip and a blade that will slit an envelope without buckling. Some examples are suggested and you might wish to modify one of these designs to suit your own ideas.

Simple types are made from brass sheet #16 or #18 gauge. You can cut a shape with a piece to roll over as shown on page 120 (top), or you could turn the end back as shown on page 120 (middle). A larger roll brought down and riveted would provide more grip.

A variation is to make the rolled-over part wider so that you can pierce a design such as an initial or emblem as shown on page 120 (bottom). You can complete an emblem by punching surface lines on it.

Making the blade

For all of these openers, while you want to thin the edges of the blade, you do not want to make a fine cutting edge, because such an edge would not last long. Take the edges fairly thin and then round them. Round all edges of the handle part. Polish all over before bending.

Sheet brass will bend easily. You can also obtain a machining-quality brass strip that is stiffer and not intended for bending, but could be used for flat letter openers. You can use $\frac{1}{16}$" or thicker strip and reduce the blade to an elliptical or diamond section while keeping the handle flat with rounded edges. Another possibility is to make a simple outline with a hole for a hanging string as shown at the top of page 121 (top), or you could pierce a design as shown at the top of page 121 (bottom).

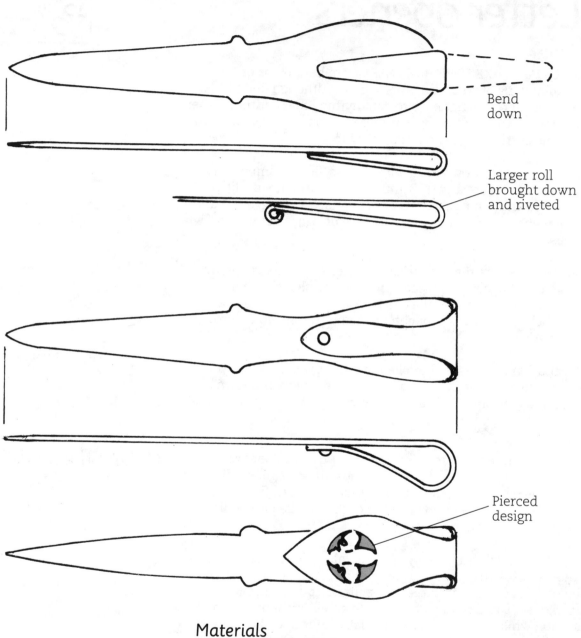

Bend
down

Larger roll
brought down
and riveted

Pierced
design

Materials
Brass sheet, #16 or #18 gauge

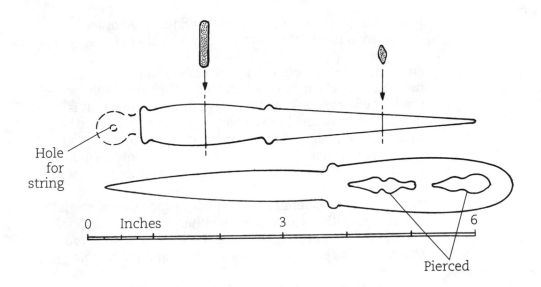

Hole
for
string

0   Inches   3   6

Pierced

Making the handle

One option for making the handle is to thicken it, which will improve grip and possibly appearance. To do this, you can add metal, wood, or hard plastic to one or both sides as shown below.

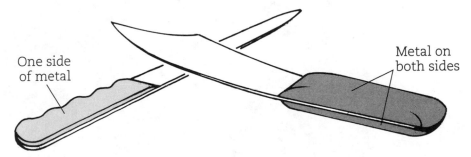

One side
of metal

Metal on
both sides

The simplest handle to make is a piece of metal on one side. This can be a color that contrasts with or complements the metal of the blade, such as copper on brass. Make the overlay slightly too large so you can file the edges level after joining. If you choose, you can include finger notches to add both character and grip.

You can soft-solder the parts by coating both meeting surfaces with solder. Apply flux, and then clip the parts together and heat until the solder surfaces melt and unite. Another possibility is to join the parts with epoxy adhesive.

Pieces of metal on both sides of the blade will offer more to hold. You could use brass for the blade, but you might prefer steel for contrast. A knife for other purposes—one that is intended to take and keep a sharp edge—would have to be made of tool steel, and then hardened and tempered. You could use tool steel, but a letter opener need only be mild steel, which is easier to work and strong enough for its purpose.

You could soft-solder brass or copper to each side of steel. You can attach (with epoxy adhesive) either wood, colored hard plastic, or metal overlays. Be sure the wood or plastic you choose is thick enough to allow you to round the handle.

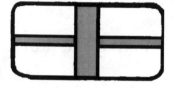

Many traditional knives have their handles riveted on. Letter opener handles do not need rivets, but if you want to give a riveted appearance you could glue in pieces of brass or copper rod as shown at left.

Spoons

SPOONS CAN BE MADE in many sizes—from quite small sugar spoons up to salad servers and ladles. The most convenient metal for working spoons is copper, but you could use gilding metal. However, these metals are unsuitable for use directly in contact with food, so you must regard copper and gilding metal spoons as purely for decoration unless you have them plated with nickel, chromium, or silver. Aluminum is a good metal with which to make larger items as shown below.

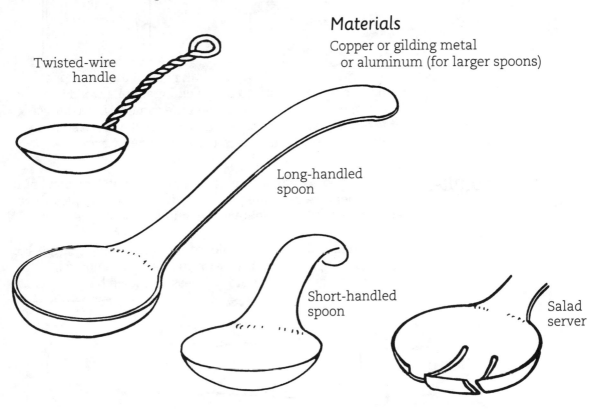

Twisted-wire
handle

Materials
Copper or gilding metal
   or aluminum (for larger spoons)

Long-handled
spoon

Short-handled
spoon

Salad
server

The bowl of a spoon is small. You could hollow it with the small end of some bossing mallets on a sandbag, but there are several other ways to hollow. For example, you could work over a hollow hammered in a lead block, as shown below (left).

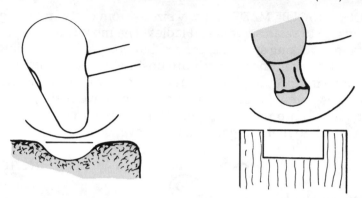

Another possibility is to use the ball peen of an engineer's hammer over a hole drilled in the end grain of a wood block as shown above (right). Action is then the same as in making a large bowl—working in circles, ellipses, or shapes to suit the spoon—but be careful to keep the small hollow even.

Integral handles

You can choose to make the handle integral with the bowl or to hard-solder on a separate piece. The following examples show techniques that you might wish to adapt to other designs.

A short-handled spoon suitable for sugar and other granules or powders (see page 123) is cut with the handle blending into the bowl with large curves to aid stiffness as shown below. Hollow

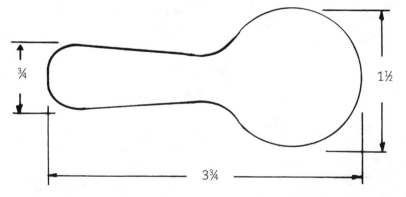

the bowl evenly and planish it. The short handle should be stiff enough without more treatment.

One way of stiffening a handle is to raise one or more bars on it, as shown below (left). Make a mild steel punch on flat strip by filing and polishing a round end, and use it with the spoon handle face-down on a lead block as shown below (right). Planish the metal outside the bar and leave final trimming of the handle to shape until all other work has been done.

Stiffening

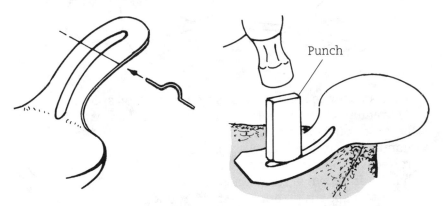

Punch

Another way to stiffen a handle is to soft-solder on an overlay as shown at right. For maximum stiffness let the point of the overlay extend into the bowl. If you like, you could add a punched design on the overlay as shown below. Bend both parts fairly close to the final shape before soldering, as a soft-solder joint might not hold together if you try to bend it much.

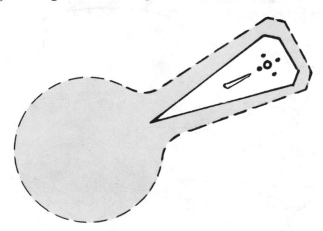

Spoons 125

Added handles

You can add a handle with a piece of stouter round or other section copper rod. Spread and thin the end to hard-solder to the bowl; the other end might be spread to a limited amount, but if you want a larger end, hard-solder one on as shown below. Yet another option is to twist wire to form a handle (see page 123) instead of making a rod handle.

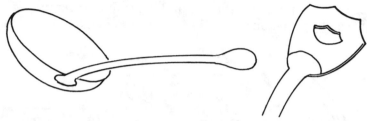

You can use the same methods for larger-sized spoons. Aluminum will make salad servers or ladles (see page 123), but because you cannot solder this metal, handle stiffness will have to come from raised bars or from hollowing the whole handle as shown at right. Ends of these and other spoons do not have to be round. You can form them elliptical or in other shapes.

One final option is to form the end into a scoop instead of into a bowl. If you need a deeper or larger scoop, you can cut and rivet corners and rivet on a stiffer handle as shown below.

Bracketed lantern

AN OUTSIDE LIGHT can be arranged in many ways. This one
has a traditional lantern appearance, that is shaped like an old-
time oil or gas lamp mounted on a wall bracket. However, it is
designed for electric light, and its construction is a combination
of sheet metalwork and simple blacksmithing as shown on
page 128.

All parts can be made of mild steel, although the lamp tube can
be a different metal. You could weld some parts, but you can
join many of them with bolts or rivets. Self-tapping, sheet-metal
screws are suitable and convenient for the thinner metal parts.

The sizes suggested (see page 129) should suit most needs. If
you want to vary the sizes, you will have to develop lantern
parts and the shape of the roof to get accurate angles and sizes.
Of course, development has been done for an assembly of the
sizes given.

You can prepare several parts in advance. If you start with the
lantern frame, followed by its roof, and then the square pad
and its scrolls to support the lantern, you can allow for slight
variations as you progress. Once you have made what the
bracket has to support, you can begin construction on the
bracket with its scrolls.

The lantern frame is built up from pieces of #18 gauge sheet
mild steel. You could make some joints with rivets, but self-
tapping screws are probably a better choice, since they can be
used everywhere. You need to drill a clearance hole in the
outer piece and a tapping hole in the inner piece. Because of
the conical shape of the frame, none of the angles are square.
Designed angles are indicated, but you can bend parts
approximately and adjust angles as you fit pieces together.

Start with the lantern bottom as shown at the top of page 130.
The central large hole provides ventilation, has enough
clearance for passing a lamp through, and allows you to put

Making the bottom

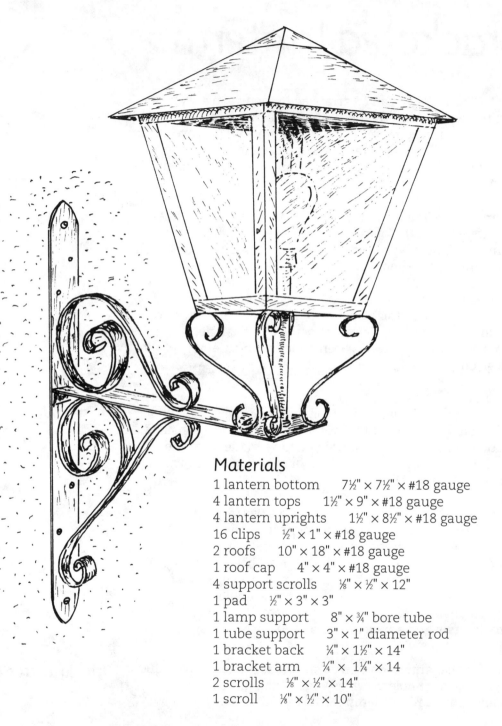

Materials

1 lantern bottom   7½" × 7½" × #18 gauge
4 lantern tops   1½" × 9" × #18 gauge
4 lantern uprights   1½" × 8½" × #18 gauge
16 clips   ½" × 1" × #18 gauge
2 roofs   10" × 18" × #18 gauge
1 roof cap   4" × 4" × #18 gauge
4 support scrolls   ⅛" × ½" × 12"
1 pad   ½" × 3" × 3"
1 lamp support   8" × ¾" bore tube
1 tube support   3" × 1" diameter rod
1 bracket back   ¼" × 1½" × 14"
1 bracket arm   ¼" × 1¼" × 14
2 scrolls   ⅛" × ½" × 14"
1 scroll   ⅛" × ½" × 10"

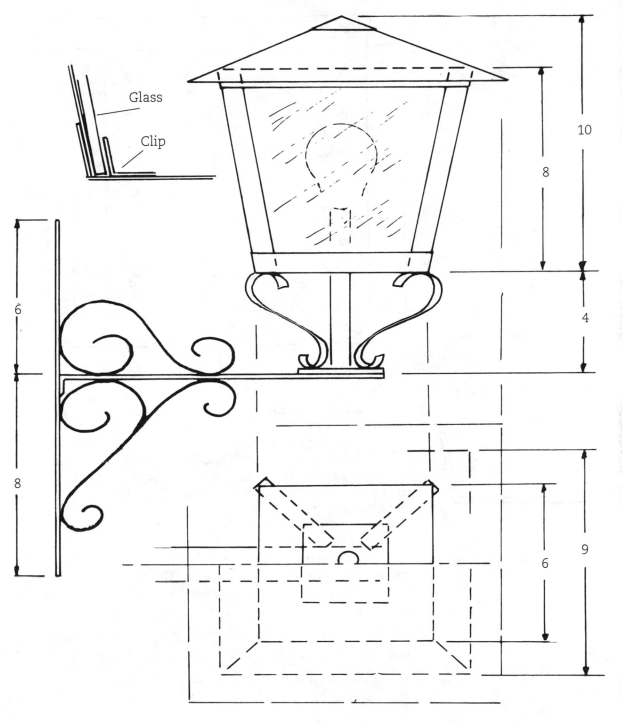

Glass

Clip

6

8

10

8

4

6

9

Bracketed lantern 129

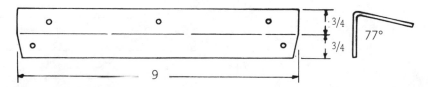

Ventilation
hole

4½

6

7½

Drill these
clearance
holes first

Holes for
glass clips

Holes for
scrolls

100°

your hand inside during construction. The cut corners flare out to 100° to match the slopes of the sides. All holes are shown, but only the end clearance holes in the flanges should be drilled at this stage. Corner holes for the scrolls and those for the glass clips can be marked, but you might need to modify their positions during assembly. Bend the flanges to 100° as shown at left.

The four top pieces have their lower leg corners sloped and drilled with clearance holes for attaching to the uprights. The top leg will have holes for screws into the roof. Mark them as a guide, but do not drill them yet. Bend these strips to 77° as shown below.

3/4

3/4

77°

9

130 *Decorative Metalworking*

The four uprights will be bent to slightly wider than square because of the assembled conical form as shown below. Cut the end angles to match the shapes of the parts they will fit into, but do not drill holes yet.

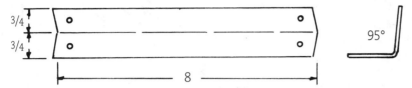

Next, put the four uprights inside the corners of the base. Mark through and drill tapping holes. Join these parts with self-tapping screws. Add top pieces outside the uprights in the same way, and check symmetry. You will get a more regular shape if you make a hardboard or plywood piece to fit in one side, and then try it at all positions. You will be able to use the shaped piece as a template for the glass.

You will need eight clips to secure the glasses inside the lantern bottom and another eight under the roof. Cut them to size and drill them as shown at right. Their bends will be flared out a little wider than square, but you can postpone adjustments until you fit the glass. Then you can bend them to fit tightly.

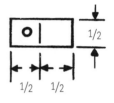

Make the lantern roof in two parts with a separate cap to avoid the difficulty of getting a close point when bending a single piece made up of all four faces. It is important that you make all four faces the same. Start by making a template of one of them, as shown at the top of page 132. Draw around this on your metal and mark a second face alongside it. Add a strip for the joint, and then make a second piece to match. Drill clearance holes for self-tapping screws.

Making the roof

When you bend the roof parts, the angle between roof faces is slight; what is important is that when the two sections are put together the lower edges form a square. The height at the center will then be about 2½ inches. When you are satisfied with the shape, screw the sections together.

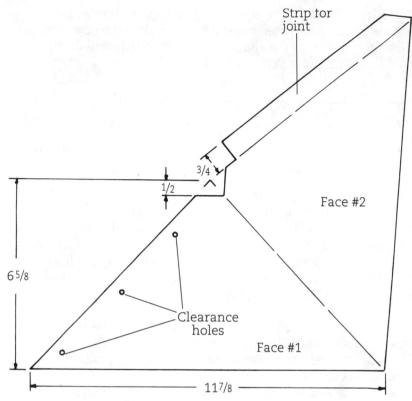

Strip for joint

3/4

1/2

6 5/8

Face #2

Clearance holes

Face #1

11 7/8

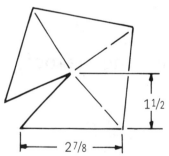

1 1/2

2 7/8

You can make the cap for the roof from a single piece of metal as shown at left. Mark this out in the same way as the roof; use a template for one face. Angles should be the same as the roof. (If necessary, modify the sizes given to suit your roof.)

Bend the cap to fit over the apex of the roof; then drill for one screw at the center of each face. Coat the underside with jointing compound and screw the cap on.

Assembling the roof

Try the assembly together. Invert it and check that the roof overhangs the same all around, and then mark the location of the top pieces of the frame on the roof. With these marks as a guide, drill screw holes in the roof. Three screws at each side should be sufficient.

Before attaching the roof, fit the glasses. You could use clear, tinted, or patterned glass. Fit clips to the lantern bottom, two at each side, and spring them to grip the glass. Fit the roof temporarily with a few screws. Then, with the assembly inverted, you can reach through and fix clips inside the roof. Spring the clips to grip the glass when you finally screw on the roof.

Before final assembly, you should paint the metal inside and out. Paint in joints will also help to delay rust. A treatment with rust-inhibiting fluid followed by two coats of paint should be satisfactory. For maximum illumination, you could paint inside the roof with aluminum paint. Outside paint could match nearby color schemes.

The lantern is supported above the bracket by four scrolls on a square pad attached to the bracket. This also takes a tube carrying the electric lamp. The scrolls are arranged diagonally to the lantern base. They are shown raising the lantern 4", but you could modify the height as shown on page 134.

Making the supports

You might have to alter the lamp support to suit your chosen lamp and its fitting. In the design, it is assumed the support is a piece of ¾" bore tube, which can be any metal. Its length has to be arranged to bring the light source to or just above the middle of the lantern. So that you will be able to remove the light assembly to replace a light bulb, the tube slides onto a support drilled through to take the cable. You will have to arrange for sufficient spare length of cable to be available to allow you to lower the lamp through the hole in the lantern bottom.

The support could be a piece of ¾" rod, but it would be better if you can turn a piece with a shoulder on a lathe as shown on page 134. You can secure the support by passing it through the pad and the bracket and then lightly riveting it underneath, or you can hard-solder it.

Make the square pad ¼" thick. Drill it for the lamp tube support, two rivets into the bracket and at the corners for ³⁄₁₆" bolts into the scrolls.

Make four identical scrolls from ⅛"-x-½" strip. Drill the ends for ³⁄₁₆" bolts. You can make a trial assembly, but delay permanent attachment until you have the bracket ready to fit to the pad and the tube support.

Making the scrolls & bracket

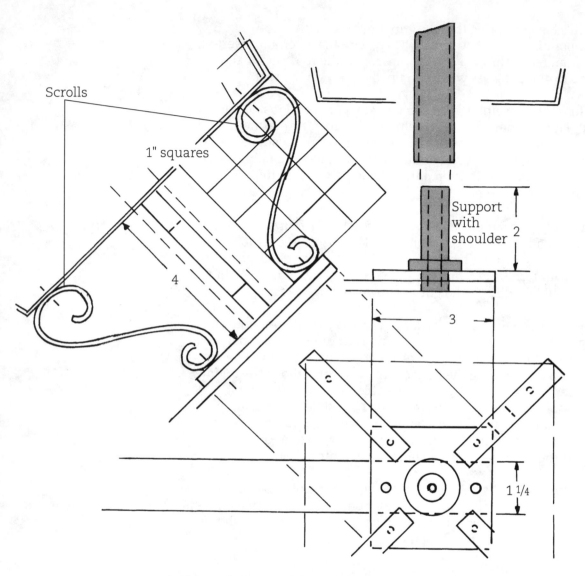

Scrolls

1" squares

4

Support with shoulder

2

3

1 1/4

The main parts of the bracket are made from ¼"-x-1¼" strip, and the scrolls are made from ⅛"-x-½" strip or larger section as shown at the top of page 135. The back is flat against the wall, but you can shape its ends as shown at the bottom (left) of page 135. Mark the position of the arm, which has to be bent and attached with two ¼" rivets or bolts as shown at the middle (right) of page 135. The pad as shown at the bottom (right) of page 135 goes at the end of the arm, and you can bolt or rivet it in place.

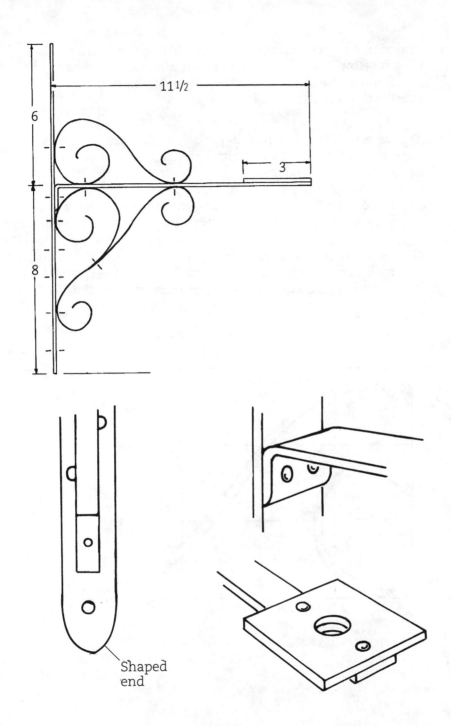

11 1/2

6

3

8

Shaped
end

Bracketed lantern 135

The scrolls for the bracket are formed to one basic outline, as shown below. Make two complete to this pattern. Repeat the small end of the scroll with sufficient length extending to overlap the complete scroll.

Final assembly

Try the scrolls in position, and mark them and the bracket parts for ³⁄₁₆" diameter fixing bolts. Arrange the extending piece so the curl comes under the end of the scroll on top and can be bolted through it. Then cut it to overlap the main scroll and bolt it there. Drill holes for attaching the lantern to the wall so the holes are clear of the scrolls. (Most load will be at the top.)

Now you can make a final assembly and paint the whole thing. You might not need to lift the tube off its support very often, but so it will come away easily you can coat the meeting parts with grease to prevent them from seizing up.

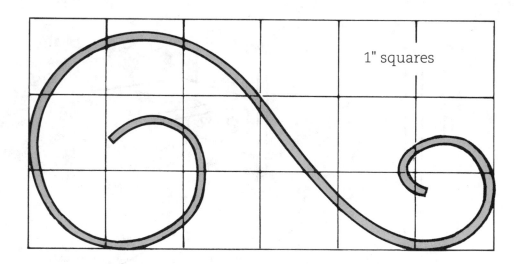

1" squares